"As one in recovery myself, I found Dr. Parker's expertise and wisdom tremendously helpful. It will help many, many lives."

Sandra Simpson LeSourd, Author,
THE COMPULSIVE WOMAN

"Dr. Parker's guidelines for recovery are clear, comprehensive and so logical ... You'll wonder why you couldn't see them before. It's a book for women *and* men."

T. A., Hampton, VA
Recovering cocaine addict

"Finally! A book about being well ... not about being sick."

R. W., Philadelphia, PA
Compulsive overeater

"I finally realized that alcohol was only one side of my problem — relationship dependencies were the other. The principles of *Deep Recovery* are helping me to succeed in my recovery from both."

C. A., Ontario, Canada

"Dr. Parker has shown me that *I* am responsible for my own recovery ... and what *I* have to do to make it happen."

E. B., Nashville, TN
"Codependent"

"An entertaining, educational and challenging voyage of self-discovery ... unlike any other recovery book I've read."

W. O., Norfolk, VA

"Now, when something "bad" happens in my life, I am able to see it as a lesson opportunity. My setbacks are fewer and farther between."

C. S., Austin, TX

DEEP
RECOVERY

*How to use your most difficult relationships
to find out who you are!*

Dr. Charles E. Parker

Hawkeye Press
Virginia Beach, Virginia

Edited by: Karen King Gulbranson

Cover design by: Bill Owen

Cover illustration by: Nick Gonzales-Goad

Hawkeye Press
Post Office Box 62547
Virginia Beach, Virginia 23462

Library of Congress Catalog Card Number: 91-73225

Publisher's Cataloging in Publication Data

Parker, Dr. Charles E.
Deep Recovery: How to Use Your Most Difficult Relationships to Find Out Who You Are / by Dr. Charles E. Parker.
Bibliography
Includes Index
1. Recovery
2. Addictions
3. Codependency
4. Self-help
5. Alcoholics — Family Relationships
LC 91-73225
ISBN 0-9629769-6-2: $12.95 Softcover

Printed in the United States of America on recycled paper.

TO

Sensei Hiroyuki Tesshin Hamada,
a man beyond time.

AND TO

The members of Honbu and Bushin Kan Dojos,
fellow students in the Way of the Lessons.

TABLE OF CONTENTS

AUTHOR'S PREFACE

At the outset, permit me to express my gratitude for having the opportunity to share my thoughts with you in these next pages. You will find that this book is an unusual mix of both new and ancient thoughts. I hope it will make a genuine contribution to your recovery process, or perhaps at least suggest a new way of viewing your life experience. It is a book that will likely be a challenge in some respects, as I have tried to include ideas that may, at first, be considered unusual for a book about relationships and recovery

In that regard, I ask for your forbearance with Chapters Two and Three, as you may not initially wish to delve so deeply into the subjects of thinking and language. As I've worked on this book over the last several years, the subjects of language and thinking have continually pressed forward in my mind as being essential ingredients for the recovery process. Therefore, in spite of their abstract nature, I have carried on with their early position in the book. If you find them ponderous, you can move right on to the practicality of Chapter Four, and return to these chapters at a later time when they may be more pertinent to your life.

Dr. Charles E. Parker
Virginia Beach, Virginia

ACKNOWLEDGMENTS

In large measure, this is not "my book." It is a condensation of observations and lessons learned from many different people, and its accuracy is confirmed by sages from the beginning of recorded history. While some contributions evolved from remote associations, others were practical, contemporary and essential to the completion of the manuscript.

In this latter regard, one person deserves credit for making this book far more readable and less ponderous than it otherwise might have been — Karen King Gulbranson. Her intelligent and insightful review and editing have decisively contributed to the flow of the manuscript and have eliminated many of the unforeseen impediments that so often forestall completion of a project this size. Karen has an unusual sense of what works on paper and what doesn't. Not only did she handle the laborious task of line editing, she also constructively contributed to issues of structure, content and style. Karen adopted this book as her own and put extraordinary hours and care into its completion.

From a more distant perspective, I am grateful to Mr. Thomas Walker, English instructor at Culver Military Academy in 1959-1960, for his encouragement and appreciation of my beginning efforts with poetry and writing. He was a considerate teacher whose balanced remarks reached across time, far beyond the classroom.

In the years that have passed since I first signed on as a Clinical Director of Adolescent Services, I have felt it a special privilege to be associated with the extended team at HCA Peninsula Hospital in Hampton, Virginia. The clinical and nursing staff, the administrative group and the dietary and housekeeping departments all make the effort to walk the extra mile for patients, even under some of the most difficult circumstances. I appreciate their encouragement and their patience as we have continued to grow together. Most especially, I appreciate their efforts at balance and their willingness to courageously address the changes that are taking place in the mental health field.

A warm thanks also to my associates at the Center for Personal Recovery in Virginia Beach for sharing their clinical experience and their observations.

Dr. Hamada, to whom the book is dedicated, taught me the most profound lessons with the fewest words. His remarks, terse and timely, were shared in the context of a variety of work-out experiences that took us from the predawn rain on Jockey's Ridge, to those cold December waterfalls and the slippery sweat of the dojo floor. The reality at first seemed different there, but in the end it was all recovery.

As you will see from some of the clinical examples, I have had the opportunity to work with many wonderful patients from all walks of life. Sharing their difficulties and observations has been the greatest privilege and has provided convincing evidence of the usefulness of the *Deep Recovery* process. I am deeply appreciative for their having been a part of my life.

Others whose insights have been integrated into the structure or content of the book are Allen Phemister, L.C.S.W., Dr. Edward DeBono, Alexandra Ahrens and Stan Hainer. Their thoughts and observations have been most appreciated. Thanks to Bill Owen for his inspired cover design and to Janet Shaughnessy for her help with the illustrations. My gratitude also goes out to Jeanine Stanley, Anne Blanchard, Barbara Perkins and Michelle Scott who helped type some of the first drafts.

A special thanks to my family. My wife, Cathy, is a full partner, both personally and professionally. Her insights, comments and business sense have been supportive and essential to the completion of the manuscript. Her practical experience has also been helpful, as she has regularly applied balance concepts in her own life. My son, Nat, and daughter, Susan, regularly share their astute, worldly perceptions and fresh perspectives with me. They often remind me of the ageless benefits of surprise and the natural creativity of youth. The depth of their observations is both shocking and reassuring.

When The Student Is Ready
The Lesson Appears

1

What You See Is What You Get:

A New Perspective

"The field cannot be seen from within the field."
Ralph Waldo Emerson

RECOVERY. BALANCE. SERENITY. WISDOM. Profound words — worthy lifetime goals. Yet, these words represent diverse concepts whose values are not easily communicated. Many of us seek daily to reach the goals represented by these words as we think about our past actions and attempt to correct our current behaviors. As time passes, we whittle away at our misunderstandings, our denial patterns and our own misperceptions. Self-observation is often tricky. It is difficult because we cannot see our patterns unless we view ourselves and our relationships from a different perspective. For it is indeed true that "the field cannot be seen from within the field."

Over time, we further discover that our lives cannot be successfully managed through the anachronistic manipulation of old concepts with words or simplistic thinking. Over time, our communication system fails, as George Orwell once observed: "If thought corrupts language, language can also corrupt thought." With the passage of years, we find that the more we think we know, the less we actually understand. And we find ourselves faced with the vexing paradox that *our greatest difficulties in life are ex-*

perienced within the context of our most important and valued relationships.

In the context of these difficulties, neither your life's time nor your important relationships can be managed successfully unless you start thinking more deeply and more comprehensively about your own life experience. As you contemplate your past experience, you'll ultimately discover that you must seek to recover from your own illusions. Every successful recovery process involves illusion recovery. Your past perceptions are distorted by your previous view. Looking at the field from within the field causes illusions, much as it did back in the days when people thought the world was flat.

During the recovery process, people often become disoriented because they are faced with a new view of the past. They find they must leave the safety of comfortable preconceptions and advance into a new territory that is both mysterious and uncharted. To think so deeply at the onset of a recovery practice often seems to be an impossible task.

Deep Recovery will show you how to make practical use of your past relationship illusions and patterns to remain in the recovery process. It is a guide to help you resolve confusions, to remove useless preconceptions, and to demonstrate useful, meaningful patterns in everyday relationship difficulties. It is a book written with a worthy purpose — to help you change your life.

RECOVERY PROBLEMS

In any recovery process, stumbling blocks inevitably arise. Despite your best efforts at "working a program" of self-discovery and self-evolution, you find that your relationship patterns, as well as your communication patterns, set you back. You become consumed by anger and/or sadness, or by the destructive patterns of control and avoidance. With any setback, you may feel even more helpless and hopeless than ever, because you "failed" in your recovery effort. You feel humiliated for ever having thought you could succeed in the first place. Your setback seems to confirm your old perception of yourself as an incompetent, or, conversely, your failures may challenge your illusion of competence.

Too quickly, you may find yourself falling back into the same old coping patterns and defensive activities that caused you so much pain in the first place. This sort of self-doubt usually occurs because people don't understand *that setbacks or relapsive behavior can be instructive and useful.*

Another commonplace recovery quandary occurs around the isolationist attitudes of some recovery groups. Each such group preaches its own reductionistic gospel of compliance and restrictive thinking and behavior. In these groups, codependents are separated from chemical dependents, drug addicts from alcoholics, IV cocaine users from cocaine smokers and celebrities from common folk. The emphasis is placed on *differences* rather than *similarities*. But, the truth is that when we are out of balance, we *all* exhibit the *same* destructive patterns. It is only in our individual human accomplishments that we are different. And just as we use our accomplishments to differentiate ourselves, we can use our troubles to understand our similarities.

A further recovery difficulty puzzles even the most experienced: *The recovery process itself is fraught with inherent theories and illusion systems that can quickly replace your former faulty illusions with new ones that may be just as limiting as the first.* Just as any new idea has its benefits, it also has its liabilities. We can get so caught up in the apparent benefits, that we overlook potential liabilities that can lead to ongoing self-victimization.

Before addressing the many subtle pitfalls of advanced recovery activity, several fundamental questions present themselves: Are there any basic concepts that can be used to evaluate one's progress in the recovery process? Is there a practical way to find and understand balance in everyday conversation? What are the early signs of self-victimization, and how can they be used to fuel the recovery process? And, most important, what does the word *"recovery"* really mean? The answers to these questions will each be specifically addressed in *Deep Recovery*.

RECOVERY

Recovery is a gradual process of transcendence, enlightenment and understanding. *It is a process of learning about, and understanding the usefulness of, the painful bumps that each of us encounters within our own experience of changing reality.* In recovery, the bumps become lessons. Recovery is a process of regular self-change. It is a process of redefining the self ... redefining who *you* are. Lexicographer Noah Webster once said, "In time, all definitions must be revised." Although Webster was referring to words, the same statement can be applied to our attitudes and values.

As we grow older, we seek wisdom in an effort to prevent further difficulties in life. In recovery, we must overcome our own short-sighted, myopic view of the world that has been fed and encouraged by our fears, our primitive defensive patterns and our mind-altering gratifications. The recovery process requires that we let go of our misperceptions, our rationalizations, our addictive patterns and our special, individualized systems of illusion. We must learn to face *every* new aspect of reality, for the recovery process is not reality selective. It neither excludes nor avoids any reality, because that type of limited thinking keeps the thinker unbalanced.

Our egos, our thinking patterns and our mental habits can keep us unbalanced in one of two ways. Either we diminish ourselves by our limited, helpless, ego-defective habits of thinking (i.e. low self-esteem), or we handicap ourselves with puffed-up, egoistic patterns like those of a cocky 17-year-old who thinks he has all of the answers (i.e. pride).

In addition, the fact that we are unaware of these patterns adds the complicating factor of *confusion*. It is our unconscious *defensive* patterns that cause our confusion during recovery. And, unless we can uncover these unconscious patterns — recognize and understand them — we will remain confused. The good news, however, is that just because such patterns are unconscious, it does not mean that they are impossible to understand. In fact, once the simplicity and pervasiveness of their expression is grasped, they are readily accessed and understood. We regularly experience awareness setbacks during the recovery process. Our awareness setbacks reveal our limited view. They encourage a change in our perception, a larger understanding of the process of our life. As we encounter each new reality, we find ourselves thinking more deeply, discovering new layers of ourselves and of the world around us. Our previous levels of comprehension and perception are challenged by each new level that is no longer cloaked in denial. But before we know it, we're confused again and in a state of mental disarray. We can't see the forest for the trees. The confusion we experience at this deeper level results from our lack of understanding of the Big Picture — our inability to make the connections between whatever difficult event we're facing and our own education, personal history and childhood lessons. Without a larger understanding, the past lessons and life experience seem disconnected from the present difficulties.

Feeling lost and alone in this new confusion, we seek comfort in the familiarity of repetitive patterns: addictions, relationship dependencies, compulsive behaviors, automatic defensive reactions. In times past, these patterns may have kept our species alive. But at this point in human development, they can completely undo us. A deep understanding of recovery will not only help you to recognize these repetitive, destructive patterns, but will also help you to correct them once they are recognized.

"ONE DAY AT A TIME"

The phrase "one day at a time" has been the battle cry of people in recovery for many years. Certainly, the phrase has been an inspiration, but it is not without negative connotations. So many in recovery repeat it with a kind of dogged determination, in a tone that seems to imply that they are hanging from a high precipice by their fingertips.

Unintentionally, the phrase can take on a negative tone. It can become an admonition or a reproach. The implied meaning is, "Hang on." *"Don't* let go." *"Don't* weaken." *"Do not* think." *"Do not* do." *"Do not* drink." *"Do not* get upset."

Words and phrases can have either negative or positive meanings depending on the perspective of the speaker and the listener. Even the seemingly harmless phrase "one day at a time" can be given a negative connotation. And researchers have found that a negative focus is itself a set-up for relapse.

"One day at a time" can be interpreted as meaning one should just "hang in there" second by second ("hang in there" meaning *don't* relapse). Given such an interpretation, the phrase becomes an admonition rather than an observation. In recovery, we must rise above the use of simple admonitions and the categorical opposites "do" and "don't do" (*"Do* stay in recovery." *"Don't* relapse."). The two are clearly connected, because if we daily practice "don't do," we will soon grow bored and revert to "do." "Don't do" invites us to think of doing. If you see a sign that says "Don't run" what do you think of? Looking at it that way, can you see that there are deeper implications of the phrase "one day at a time"? Of the entire recovery process? *Deep Recovery* will show you the way out of "do" and "don't do." *Deep Recovery* rises above the simplistic labels of positive and negative categories.

If "one day at a time" is not an *admonition* against the drudgery, boredom and mayhem of life, what other meaning can it have? Some say it is a reminder to "work your program." But isn't that just another vague suggestion? Does "work your program" mean "go to meetings" or "read about recovery"? Others closer to the deeper spiritual reference suggest that "one day at a time" is a reminder to detach and let go of the variety of attachments present in everyday life.

PAY ATTENTION

In the final analysis, "one day at a time" suggests a simple, fundamental activity that must be regularly practiced in order to remain in the recovery process — *paying attention.* When placed in this context, the phrase "one day at a time" is neither a negative reproach nor a futile, whiny moan. It is a crisp, simple reminder to pay attention — one day, one moment, one second at a time. Pay attention regularly and consistently. Always be mindful of your self-developmental process. Practice self-observation. Be as aware as you were the first time you experienced pain. Watch yourself and your reactions to your world. For the rest of your life, never let your attention lapse. Always remember that you are responsible for yourself, and that non-awareness brings additional pain. Each day, you will learn more and more about the parts of your inner and outer self that you have denied and neglected. As you continue, in recovery, to peel away the layers of limited vision, you will be regularly reminded of the profound importance of the awareness process.

Deep Recovery is a guide to help you become aware and pay attention. It will give you the specific advice you need to remain in recovery day in and day out ... moment to moment. It will show you how to recognize, within your own mind and developing value system, that you are on track. It will teach you how to pay attention and, more importantly, *what* to pay attention to. It will show you how to use the painful relationship lessons of your life for your own self-development. And, you will learn how paying attention to yourself can eliminate many of your difficulties.

The next two chapters of this book *go to the basic core of recovery.* They address the two sources of greatest confusion for us: Our thinking and our language. From there, we'll take a look at ways to deal with the patterned dependency and counterdependency responses that we have all come to use in both our individual and group relationships, and we'll review the childhood origins of our dependency patterns. Only then, will we be ready to discuss the different aspects of the recovery process and some of the difficulties found within it. The final chapter will show you how new leadership opportunities become a natural extension of your recovery process.

GETTING STARTED IN RECOVERY

Let's assume you have been in some sort of pain. Maybe it has manifested itself as a drug or alcohol addiction, or maybe as an unhealthy dependence on another person. It doesn't really matter. What matters is the pain you feel. Your recovery process begins the minute you look around to see what has happened to you and how you might avoid it in the future. One of the most difficult initial discoveries is that you have, in fact, caused much of your own pain. Through growing self-awareness, you will begin to attempt to use the lessons of your past to prevent further pain from occurring. The recovery process is an ongoing self-awareness process. Therefore, any effort at self-awareness is an effort at recovery.

You are probably wondering how much time and effort this recovery process is going to take. The answer is that recovery is an ongoing, never-ending process. At first, it requires more concentration because you are changing the way you view the world. Over time, it will become natural and require less effort. It will not take long for you to realize that if you do not consistently pay attention and remain aware of the way in which natural law works, you will soon be back in pain. The only real payoff for your effort and your increased awareness is diminished pain. You cannot run away from pain, but you can learn to adjust to it and to use it to learn more about the *process* of your own life.

RELATIONSHIPS

We learn the most essential lessons about our lives through our experiences with relationships. Indeed, our relationships are the windows through which we can peek into our own souls. Yet, understanding *how* we learn from such experiences can be confusing.

The relationship lessons we learn come from a combination of what others teach us (external) and what we teach ourselves (internal) through the validation of our personal experiences. Over time, the integration of external and internal information helps us begin to form more consistent patterns of self-management, as we slowly discover how to diminish our relationship difficulties.

Those people we love, care for or respect — our mentors, if you will — provide the external information that helps teach us to manage our relationships. There are three types of information they share with us:

1. *Information about others.* This type of information teaches us how to avoid or control other people by categorizing them by nationality, race, sex or religion. Such observations are inherently superficial and limited by cognitive categories, often emphasizing either the positive or negative stereotypes associated with each category. They are seductively simplistic. They encourage the beliefs that you can manipulate others, that others are different from you and that you can find ways to handle other people so that you are more comfortable. This type of information may have some limited, short-term usefulness, but it wears thin over time if used as the fundamental method for coping with, or learning from, relationships.

2. *Information about yourself.* This is the information, or feedback, others give you about what you do well and what you do poorly. Unfortunately, it is often lopsided and either inappropriately supportive or inappropriately destructive. While some significant people in your life may see you as wonderful and without fault, others may see you as inadequate and without value. We often screen information about ourselves depending on the highs and lows of our self-esteem. If we're feeling good about ourselves, we're likely to hear only the positive feedback. When we're feeling down, we may hear only criticism. Nevertheless, this type of information can be very beneficial when given and received objectively and unemotionally. It helps us develop our own internal awareness system which, in turn, helps us identify when we are creating our own problems. Evolved mentors will give you balanced observations. Those not in recovery render unbalanced, reductionistic observations.

3. *Information About All Human Beings.* This type of information helps us recognize fundamental human patterns, and it encourages respectful self-protection and harmonious balance between oneself and others. It allows us to leave our view of the field and see more clearly with Big Picture awareness. The patterns of human relationships have been present since before recorded history. Thousands of years ago, wise teachers encouraged ongoing awareness of these patterns as a way to contribute to internal balance. *Deep Recovery* will help connect these ancient observations with your everyday relationship experiences to aid your success with ongoing self-management.

Just as important as the information we receive from others is the information we internally confirm for ourselves. Over a lifetime, such information becomes progressively more valuable in the process of self-management. Slowly, our internal awareness and external lessons begin to harmonize. As we grow older, we find that some of our most difficult relationship experiences have contributed most significantly to our internal information system. Painful events increasingly teach us to pay more attention to our own experiences than to what others tell us.

Your internal information is stored in an intrinsic monitoring system that alerts you to forthcoming relationship trouble. It acts as an internal "cosmic horn" that honks to alert you when you begin to fall off the edge of awareness and balance. It honks when you're about to set yourself up for relationship troubles. Ever hear people comment that a voice told them they shouldn't get married as they walked down the aisle? However, this "horn" only works if you respect it and pay attention to it. You have to listen for it. If you don't, you will be doomed to remain in relationship difficulties. We each have the choice of ignoring or recognizing our own cosmic horns. We must separate our own internal awareness system from our childhood programming. If we hear our horn, then we must choose if we will actually listen to it. Listening does require a certain discipline, and that's why so many simply ignore their horns. But over time, we recognize that the natural price we pay for non-awareness and non-attention is more pain.

Pay attention to your cosmic horn. It's a simple plan for life. Pay attention consistently and your internal information system will slowly synchronize itself with your relationship experiences and information from other sources.

Deep Recovery will show you how to respect your cosmic horn which, in turn, will show you how your relationship difficulties can teach you about your own limited awareness of the natural world order. Ultimately, relationship problems will become your fundamental lesson plan for self-awareness — for finding out who *you* are.

Over 2,500 years ago,the Greeks engraved two simple phrases on the stone at the Oracle of Delphi:

"Know Thyself"
and
"To Thine Own Self Be True"

Your relationship difficulties can help you come to hear your own true horn. Through your own horn, you can come to know your self.

THE PROCESS AS DISCIPLINE

Your cosmic horn is your own built-in way of keeping your recovery process on track. That horn, a manifestation of your own internal teaching system, will keep you naturally aware. If you give that teaching system a chance and continue to pay attention to the self-regulatory lessons it offers, you can use it for your own self-development. In a sense, balanced recovery can give you an advanced degree in self-management. After a period of ongoing recovery practice, leadership opportunities will seem to appear from nowhere as others will attempt to learn your secrets. So, rather than you chasing success and responsibility, opportunities will come to you.

The imperative foundation for recovery lessons is found in our human relationships. They teach us about recovery, self-development and self-management. If we can't understand our unbalanced relationships, our ability to fully recover is diminished.

Any effort at recovery or responsible self-regulation is worthwhile. If an alcoholic stops drinking, that effort is certainly laudable and should be appreciated. But, in order for that alcoholic to progress to a more comprehensive recovery, he or she must first understand the feelings, insecurities and perplexing communications that occur in human relationships. Without a full understanding, the recovery focus (and effort) will consist of simply stopping that one self-destructive behavior. *Deep Recovery* will help you to achieve that understanding and to show you how individuals can use their previous destructive relationship patterns as an internal foundation upon which he or she may grow as a person.

The most successful recovery programs, such as Alcoholics Anonymous or Narcotics Anonymous, already know and utilize the process of balanced relationships. This book is *not* to be considered as a replacement or alternative for those individuals already making progress in any other recovery effort. It has been written to serve as an additional resource to those individuals who find themselves confused or stuck at any level of recovery. It offers some different insights that can *supplement,* not *replace* other recovery activities. Hopefully, it will help you see the usefulness of problems and the true value of recovery from relationship difficulties.

THE DENIAL PROCESS

Denial is a "mental hut" that we erect to keep us from paying attention to relationship reality. It is a safe closet where you can temporarily hide and pretend that something in your experience does not matter. It shrouds your unbalanced thought and communication processes. Over time, closets of denial collect considerable baggage. A collection of trash in any closet can ultimately ignite and engulf an otherwise ordinary life. Denial is a disconnection, and through it you will remain isolated and alone. In one sense, the next two chapters on thinking and language are about the pervasiveness and subtlety of the denial process. If denial flourishes, your awareness is limited. Only with the broadening of your awareness, can you contribute to your own self-healing and that of those around you.

In this day of satellite television and instant replay, we can, from our own living rooms, watch anything from a football's slow-motion bounce across the goal line, to a 2,000-pound bomb streaking through the door of a Scud missile site. You might say that technology and instant replay are keeping us increasingly honest. Through our scientific developments, we come to see ourselves more precisely. In that respect, the television is a group mirror through which we have an opportunity to see more deeply into ourselves.

The earth is not flat, nor is it the center of the universe. Through science, our field of vision has been remarkably expanded. However, through that same science, we are also learning that we can no longer remain passive with our technology. We now find that we cannot rely on science, nuclear technology, plastics or pesticides to save our relationship with our planet or with our fellow humans. Science has allowed us to step out of our earth-bound field of awareness, and it has enabled us to see our human field in the context of the universe. Through our communication system, we can now begin to leave our old limited world view — the field of our preconceptions.

Our advanced system of communication demonstrates each day how we are our own worst enemies. More and more, we recognize how we are destroying ourselves and others with our fixed thinking and our primitive, repetitive patterns. Our technologies are teaching us about ourselves. Addictions, racism and holy wars are not new problems. They are ancient safety patterns that no longer work as this small planet becomes more crowded. Individuals, like nations, find themselves ready for the truth at rates that vary according to their own denial systems (imagine the political problems that would occur if the entire world watched the same television programs). While our global communication process slowly crawls along at a path toward improved truth (an objective assessment of reality), we find ourselves increasingly self-reflective and responsible for our own personal psychological "technology."

We have decided to pay attention. By watching our personal "instant replays," we will learn to recognize when we behave wisely and with serenity. We will learn to relate in harmony with our fellow humans and the larger natural order. And we learn when we have diminished ourselves with frozen words and Paleolithic thought patterns.

In summary then, this is a book about nature and humanity, ourselves and our companions. It is a book of description, but most often one of metaphors — of word pictures. It is a book of stories that condenses many aspects of life into useful new fields of perception. It is a practical guide for finding the opportunities that arise from relationship difficulties.

Before we begin our lessons, let me share a story about some aspects of becoming a student: There is an old Zen tale about a kendo student who entered the training hall for his first lesson in the way of the sword. The aged Master stood waiting in the training hall. Dressed in full armor, his bamboo sword was poised at the ready position. The student slowly entered, dragging his armor and sword behind him on the floor.

"I'm ready for lesson one," the student said. Bam! In a flash, the Master hit him across the chest and sent him sprawling back against the wall with his equipment flying everywhere.

"That's lesson one," said the Master. "Don't come in here without your equipment on."

The Master was in tune with the natural larger order of the way things are. If you see yourself as a student, and yet are not prepared for surprises, you will have more surprises than you would ever wish for. Relationship surprises are a window into the natural Balance Order. Surprises remind you to pay attention and take you away from your past illusions. Properly understood, they teach you about your innate internal equipment.

From our western perspective, this kendo lesson may seem harsh, but the Master did no bodily harm, and the blow was a lesson in preparedness. It was a lesson in respect and self-protection that put an end to the student's innocence. It was, in that respect, a kindness. Now that you have survived your lessons, you can learn from them.

Reality, the real world, is full of useful surprises. The inevitable surprises can connect your past and your present, your inner and outer reality. This book will wake you up to that natural order and show you how to recognize the equipment you already have. Relationship difficulties will be your new training ground.

What is man's chief enemy? Each man is his own.
Anacharsis
Scythian Philosopher, 600 B.C.

2

Thinking And The Puzzle Of Natural Reality:

Your Thought Patterns Can Inhibit Your Progress

Harry Truman, Doris Day, Red China, Johnnie Ray,
South Pacific, Walter Winchell, Joe DiMaggio,
Joe McCarthy, Richard Nixon, Studebaker, Television,
North Korea, South Korea, Marilyn Monroe,
Rosenbergs, H Bomb, Sugar Ray, Panmunjam,
Brando, The King and I, and The Catcher in the Rye ...

We didn't start the fire
It was always burning
Since the world's been turning.
No we didn't light it
But we tried to fight it.

Billy Joel, Singer / Songwriter

OUR LIVES ARE A PUZZLE. Our past is a puzzle. As we look over the fragments of our past, both our personal recollections and the collective history of humankind, we find ourselves often confused. We're confused about our relationships, what they have meant in the past and what they mean today. We are perplexed about what each past event or person can teach us about today, this moment, and our next action. At times, past events seem irrelevant to the complexity of today. At other times, we blame the past for the difficulties we face today.

We didn't start the fire. We didn't start the process of change over time. *But still, we go on trying to fight it.*

Most of our confusion in life stems from our personal relationships — both past and present. Yet, in those real relationships exists our greatest opportunity for understanding the puzzles of personal growth and development. We know that we can grow from relationships, but we are also frightened of the dangers that exist when important relationships become problematic. Because, in fact, *our most important and intimate relationships* often present the most difficult challenge. Each human being, each event and each moment of personal interaction that we experience can quickly become confusing, painful and frustrating.

Serious relationship conflicts can result in arguments or fights and, on a larger scale, war and death. Difficulties in relationships may keep us locked in a living death — a stasis and emotional imprisonment from which we can't escape. Yet paradoxically, many of those same relationships offer the potential for safety, love, appreciation and comfort. So we spend our lives going up and down on a seesaw of relationship emotions that are often out of balance.

These observations aren't new at all. To be honest, they're common knowledge. What *is* new is that we can now learn to understand *why* our relationships are so difficult. To do that, we must start with a process of stepping outside of our own perceptions and limited awareness. We must look at the Big Picture beyond our own confusion ... beyond our current difficulties. Indeed, we must review our own history as a species. Peeling away the contemporary layers of space travel and laser surgery, we must delve deeper into the *defensive* activities characteristic of humanity from our earliest beginnings — even before we became Homo sapiens. For if we can understand how we have survivied the challenges of time, we can begin to see how we shoot ourselves in the foot.

HISTORICAL PERSPECTIVE: NATURAL REALITY

The history of humanity reveals a Big Picture of balance in which patterns of natural change transcend our defensive efforts. Natural patterns of change are beyond our ability to alter them. We have, for millennia, struggled to change these patterns and conquer nature. It has been in an adversarial role with nature that we have achieved our limited "success" as a species, a fact which can help us understand our problems today.

The human race has spent hundreds of thousands of years at war with its natural environment. Through our awareness of the world around us and our ability to communicate with our fellow humans, we have sought to both *control* and *avoid* nature. These conflicting desires to control and avoid reality have been the source of our greatest accomplishments ... and of our greatest undoing.

The realities of nature — the rain, sunshine, climate and seasonal variations — have challenged us to protect ourselves from natural change. Even primitive humans found caves and other forms of shelter to cope with winter cold and summer heat. They adapted to the fact that *natural reality is always undergoing change.* Rain falls, forests burn, earthquakes and hurricanes leave trails of destruction. These phenomena remind us that nature can, and often does, change very quickly and that it is truly beyond our control. As we temporarily *manage* nature, we appear to *control* it. With fire to heat and language to build shelter, we appear to have come in from the rain.

From the micro levels of nuclear particle physics to our conceptualizations of the macrocosmic universe, we humans have always studied the process of change that exists in nature. Through the enhanced perceptions of scientific technology, we have discovered that the *ongoing process of an ever-changing universe is an inarguable fact.* We have come to recognize that the physical universe is constantly changing and is, most often, *beyond our control.*

In interesting contrast, most of the history of humankind, from earliest stone age to contemporary times, has revealed increasing efforts to protect ourselves from natural change by working *against* nature. Our heat and our shelters are only temporary, short-term solutions that lead to our illusions of permanence and mastery. As technology has improved, we have developed higher levels of "defensive" management of nature. As we have found new means of control and avoidance, we have found greater freedom from those natural changes that make us uncomfortable. And, as the physical universe has continued to change, we have continued in our attempts to *use* nature to protect ourselves *from* it.

We have evolved from a world of huts and caves to one of skyscrapers, air conditioning and nuclear power. Our huts have become corporate towers; our fires are now microwave ovens.

At one time, the Native American Iroquois had only bark homes and fires to protect themselves from the harsh New England weather. Today, many New Englanders simply jet off to the Florida Keys and forget that winter exists. We're more comfortable today, because *we have, to some degree, manipulated the environment.* Such manipulation is an obvious *avoidance* of a natural reality. I am not, of course, asserting that it is *bad* to avoid natural reality and fly to Florida. But I do suggest that we have become psychologically accustomed, through positive reinforcement, to the notion that *avoidance* and *control* — the *manipulation* of natural change — are good simply because *they can make us temporarily more comfortable.*

Our ability to consistently manipulate over time has, in fact, been an important element in the survival of humankind. We, as a developing species, have to some extent rewarded, encouraged, and promoted avoidance and control since the earliest dawn of civilization and the beginning of language. Aided by our languages, we have sought increasing degrees of comfort, and we have been relatively successful in manipulating natural reality to that end.

What we seek is consistency. What we fear is change. In a situation where there is no consistency, we become uncomfortable, and we may seek control as a means to make the naturally changing order consistent.

For example, the dams on the Missouri River have been built to *control* the spring floods. That *controlling* action is a direct affront to the natural reality of the river. Or, as in the previous example of the New England winters, we may contrive to *avoid* the natural change in the climate and, thereby, create the comfort of consistency. We move to the South to *avoid* harsh winters. *Avoidance* is a form of manipulation.

Over time, however, *we must come to accept the fact that natural change consistently exists independent of our own thoughts, actions and limited perceptions.* The spring floods continue in spite of dams; winter exists in spite of Florida. Yes, we have achieved a measure of safety. Control and avoidance can work in certain respects, but natural cycles do, nevertheless, endure. Natural consistency and natural cycles continuously express themselves in spite of our efforts to alter or change them.

In some respects, human evolution has been an illusion. We modern men and women are not really so much different from our primitive ancestors. It's true that we have been somewhat successful over time in using natural substances to protect ourselves from natural events. But at the same time, we have failed miserably in our efforts to protect ourselves from our own destructive drives and from each other.

As a race, we continue to experience profound difficulties in our attempts to manage our own interpersonal (not to mention international) relationships. Our understanding of the dynamics of relationships is far behind the level of physical comfort we've achieved. We can manipulate the natural world, but we can't manage ourselves.

Because we have achieved this sense of apparent consistency, what we fear most is rapidly changing reality. Reality that changes quickly and is beyond our control or avoidance gives us fewer opportunities to make the necessary emotional and practical safety adjustments. We have become emotionally attached to the apparent consistency of the way things have been, and we are, therefore, overwhelmed by the way things are changing at this moment. Our emotional, and much of our intellectual, lives are tied to the drive for order and consistency in this ever-changing physical universe. But, on the other hand, with consistency can come boredom, and boredom can be as devastating as change. The conclusion is irrefutable. Most of humanity is caught between boredom and fear of change.

Down through eons, we have been trained to perceive change as being dangerous. We associate change with pain. And, because we are still emotionally unprepared for change, we can't understand it. Nor can we synchronize ourselves with the larger natural order of change that we regularly experience on a smaller scale in our relationships. On the one hand, we continue to overreact to change, on the other, we believe we are above it.

Toiling on the treadmill of life we hide from the lessons of nature. We seek to establish a narrow lane between ourselves and the feathery zeros we dare to call angels, but ask a partition of infinite width to show the rest of creation its proper place.
John Muir, Naturalist

PSYCHIC REALITY

Natural cycles are real. They are essentially unchangeable by what we do to them or how we perceive them. Our minds cannot change them, and they exist in spite of our limited personal vision of how the world works. Natural cycles and natural phenomena have an inherent balanced reality that is independent of our mental manipulations.

In a similar way, each of us has our own naturally occurring set of cycles and our own set of perceptions. We each have our own discreet *psychic reality.* These individual perceptions, or "mental huts" are real, and they serve a limited function for each of us.

Our trouble begins when we superimpose our own limited perceptions — our mental huts — over the world as it actually is. Not only do we superimpose ourselves on nature, as manifested by our disregard for planet Earth, but we do this with our fellow humans, as well. Just as we use our logical minds to convince ourselves that endangered natural species and great forests aren't particularly significant, we use our logic to diminish our fellow humans. We perceive ourselves as unique and have allowed it to go to our heads. Consequently, *we* have become the endangered species.

Once, many years ago, I debated with one of my psychoanalytic supervisors about what was "real" for a particular patient. I saw the patient's reality as my own — through *my* eyes and *my* perceptions. My supervisor argued that "there is no reality other than each individual's psychic reality."

Although I disagreed with the supervisor's observation at the time, over the years it has made increasing sense. Now I can see that each of us experiences reality differently, according to our individual psychic perceptions and our individual experience. Each of us has a separate reality. *Our perceptions — our mental huts — separate us from nature, from each other, and from an awareness of ourselves.*

Of course, there is an external, physically measurable and relatively fixed reality. Take, for example, a table and chairs. They look real. They are fixed and consistent. But, from any single person's perspective, even that relatively fixed reality may be different than it is from anyone else's. Our emotions color our view of the world. A chair may have different meanings for different individuals. Such a seemingly simple object can connote patterns of taste, power, wealth, sophistication, cleanliness, strength, sexuality or education, as it takes different psychic forms for different people. The same chair may be regarded as trash or as a throne through the power of individual psychic reality.

To further complicate matters, each reality (such as the chair) is constantly undergoing change as each person's perceptions mature and change. In other words, what you liked yesterday, you may not like today. The same chair may have many meanings over a lifetime. Likewise, a mountain or forest may have many meanings, depending upon individual needs and perceptions.

My supervisor helped me see that individuals view any given issue or object with *perceptual screens*. The mind itself alters reality by psychically screening it out or altering it through denial and avoidance.

Human emotions distort our perceptions of reality to make it more comfortable. *Thus, our psychic perceptions become our internal and external reality.* And each person becomes a complicated island of reality with his or her own unique perceptions, misconceptions and prejudices. So in a purely operational sense, each person manifests a separate reality.

THE PROBLEM WITH PSYCHIC REALITY

Imagine what happens when our perceptual screens are applied to our interactions with others. Are you beginning to understand the dilemma of human relationships? Not only must we deal with a universal, ever-changing physical reality, but as humans, we must also deal with an infinite number of interpersonal psychic realities *that not only may be different for each person, but may be changing for each other person at rates different than our own.*

Natural external variables (temperature, sunlight) on the macrovisual, easily measurable level are, in fact, relatively consistent over time. We have come to adjust to these natural variables somewhat and, as a result, we are able to design calendars, predict tidal variations, etc.

Our subatomic world is constantly changing and in motion, as well. But its changes aren't a conscious bother, because we can't perceive them, any more than we can perceive the energy in that chair which is regularly rearranging itself.

When we introduce the concept of human *psychic* reality, which may undergo multiple, rapid changes, the variables in interpersonal relationships become infinitely more complicated. Relationships often change more quickly than the weather. Difficult life situations associated with changes in relationships are often disconcerting and, at times, terrifying. They may be more frightening than death itself.

There is a story told by the troops of General J.M. Wainwright, who survived the infamous Japanese death march of Bataan in World War II. A top sergeant, it was said, climbed up on a water tower to address the troops as they were about to depart on that seemingly impossible march.

"Let me remind you," the sergeant said, "that according to the Geneva convention, they can *kill* you, but they can't *eat* you."

Small comfort, right? But the fact was that being a victim of cannibalism was a psychic reality worse than death for those soldiers. Reality is all relative. As a further example, it is well known that public speaking is the number one national fear, another "fate worse than death." In fact, death was rated as only number four in a recent list of things that frighten people (no, cannibalism wasn't on that particular list).

A further difficulty with psychic reality is the unmapped territory of personal attachment. Even ancient tribal boundaries had signs or obvious markings. But, our psychic boundaries are unmarked territories for each of us that can only be identified through information and language exchange. Our territorial attachments are pervasive and may range from objects, to people and remembered events, all of which become invested with varieties of emotional importance. There are unique, specific territories, boundaries and attachment hierarchies within each of our minds. We each have these "personal territories," and yet we often offer no maps to guide others through them. We often assume that our territories match everyone else's. But, the things we identify with and claim in our territory are different for each of us. Note, for example, the frequent use by some of the word "my": "my chair," "my house," "my program," "my team," "my unit," "my employees," "my company." The word "my" indicates a mental operation of attachment and possessiveness toward people and objects that none of us can truly own. Ownership and territory are, in fact, always changing in this world of impermanence. In a world of natural change, attachments are our amulets, our good luck charms, against impermanence. "He who dies with the most toys wins."

BALANCE: RELATIONSHIP REALITY

We are, as a species, in the midst of a new frontier, looking for a unified field theory of human relationships. Each new relationship is a new reality, as uncharted as the Yukon and as difficult to locate as an electron. The pervasiveness of our attachments, the capriciousness of our emotions, the regularity of denial and avoidance, and the natural elements of ongoing mental change have all complicated and increased relationship variables.

This new frontier is difficult to explore because the variables involved appear to be beyond measures of causality and beyond conventional means of conception. Our relationship realities are, in a way, similar to atomic physics in that we can't see what's going on, and yet certain rules do seem to apply.

As we have come to conceptualize aspects of reality and the order of the natural universe, it is interesting that we continue to be unable to grasp the natural changing order of our relationship realities. We must come to understand the changing natural reality of our relationships, just as we have come to understand the cycles of the temperature and rainfall.

Relationships respond poorly and inefficiently to our desire to manipulate through the "logic" of avoidance and control. At the most basic level, we simply can't alter other people. And if we attempt to, we pay a price. That's because other people, like the weather, are beyond our ability to change. Only they can change themselves.

In actuality, our relationships follow a natural, Balanced Order based upon the following points:

1. Within our hearts, at an almost subconscious level, we seek ways to connect — to balance and harmonize ourselves with nature and others.

2. We have an innate internal value system which signals us when we disconnect from the balanced, integrated natural order.

3. The limited gratification of *control* over nature and other people is only a temporary consolation against

the experience of vulnerability to the process of natural change.

4. Out of fear, we temporarily *avoid* change by binding ourselves in time and by diminishing our exposure to new realities.

5. Control and avoidance can work for short periods, but, over a lifetime, we come to recognize how little we can control and how little we can avoid.

6. Gratifications that alter awareness and perception of reality (alcohol, drugs, sex, etc.) can only serve as temporary insulation against the ultimate awareness of change.

7. Until we are alone with our own pain, created by our own limited awareness, we are not motivated to see more deeply into the natural order of things.

8. Our most basic pain comes from emotional conflicts in the face of natural relationship elements that are unavoidable and beyond our control.

9. Our greatest opportunity for daily enlightenment, for the practice of natural balance, lies within the mirror of our most important relationships.

10. Our greatest satisfactions in life come not from accolades or awards, but from our growing inner awareness of self-mastery with each new level of responsibility.

11. These are lessons that we can only learn through our own personal life experience and in our relationship with our own true self — the self of natural values.

12. These lessons are regularly repeated throughout life, and they will continue to be repeated regardless of our attitude or attention to the process.

METACOMMUNICATION

The Balance Order is patterned, coded, and initially difficult to penetrate and understand without the use of metaphors and metacommunication. Metacommunication is simply a means of communication and explanation that goes beyond ordinary thinking and talking. It is a type of communication that goes beyond "either/or," dualistic thinking and, at the same time, *includes* that very kind of thinking in an effort to see the whole picture. It is a way of describing what reality really is, not what we interpret it or perceive it to be. It is a reality beyond psychic reality ... beyond our own personal distortions.

The Balance Order requires some broad thinking on a level above superficial observation of behavior. But once understood and visualized, it is as predictable as the tides. To see this Balance Order, we must step outside the rose-colored dreams, perceptions and interpretations that guide us through most of our lives. We must awaken and take a courageous, creative leap out of our desire for comfort and consistency. Only then, can we *begin to see the natural order consistency as it actually exists in each one of us.*

The natural order is often independent of our will or our thoughts. To understand it, we must rise above our fears. To recognize it, we must rise above our desire for gratification and safety. In a sense, we have to leave the shelter of our logical minds in order to find it. We must leave the "mental huts" we have constructed for ourselves over the millennia of human history. Metaphor and the process of metacommunication help us to do it.

If I suggested through a metaphor, for example, that the August sun is a lion, you might argue with me about it. After all, the sun has no hair, a lion is a mammal, etc. But, there are certain characteristics of each entity that can creatively, through one's imagination, be connected. Close your eyes for a moment and imagine that hot August sun silently stalking you, ferocious in its yellow brilliance. Can you see the connection?

The sun and the lion are indeed separate entities, but this metaphoric connection of the two gives them both a new and different conceptual manifestation. Such a metaphoric remark *includes observable aspects of each entity but is different than each.* This particular metaphor is a metacommunication about the intensity of the August sun.

In his book *Maps of the Mind,* psychologist Charles Hampden-Turner discusses the concept of metacommunication by using the riddle of the Sphinx, which is itself a metaphor.

According to the riddle, the Sphinx, which you may know is a mythical combination of a woman, a lion and a bird, stood guard on the road leading to the ancient city of Thebes. As travelers approached, the Sphinx threatened to kill them if they could not solve the following riddle: What walks on four legs in the morning, two legs at noon and three legs in the evening?

One day, Oedipus came along. He was able to answer the riddle correctly because he had an understanding of deeper level metacommunication and the use of metaphor in language. Have you figured it out? The correct answer is "Man."

By transcending the simple, concrete use of the word "legs," as well as the traditional concept of what constitutes a "day," Oedipus recognized that man walked (crawled) on "four legs" as a child in his early days, on two legs in the middle of his life and on three legs (with a cane) in old age. Thus, in this metaphoric representation, the "day" that the Sphinx asked about was really the entire human lifetime, and the interpretation of the word "legs" included arms and a walking stick.

So it is that in order to understand the Balance system, we must allow ourselves to think on a level of metacommunication and metaphor — of deeper reality and of meanings beyond the apparent and completely logical order. Metacommunication is inclusive and connective. Ordinary thought is exclusive and disconnective. In fact, metacommunication involves the processes of *both* logical and metaphoric thought.

BALANCE

The Balance process involves learning in a different way from what we are used to. As Gregory Bateson points out in *Steps to an Ecology of Mind,* this learning involves more than simple rote memory. It is more complicated than content-focused learning by choice among several variables or sets of variables. Indeed, Balance is a change in the *pro-*

cess of how we learn — a change in the *system of sets of alternatives*. It's moving conceptually from which car you buy to how you buy a car. It is a different way of approaching the self-development process and of reframing the perceived order. It includes not only what we can see (content), but also the *process* of how we *arrange* or *rearrange* what we see.

Metaphors crystalize many diverse elements. They are, in a sense, a new field of reality, a field larger than simple, denotative word representations. Metaphors are language fields that can stretch across boundaries of space and time to connect a variety of apparently disconnected elements. Metacommunications are shared observations that, just as metaphors, transcend reality in such a way that they can be appreciated from a larger, more comprehensive perspective.

Field theory states that there is no exact position of an electron — that it exists in a "field" (the Heisenberg Uncertainty Principle). As this theory is useful to nuclear particle physics, the metaphor is useful to appreciate the larger perspective of the grey areas in communication. Metaphors bridge the gap between diacritic and synesthetic thinking. *Diacritic* thinking is predominantly left brain and dualistic. It is focused on content. It separates things so that they can be discriminated and managed appropriately. This type of thinking groups items into conceptual entities even though they are, individually, somewhat different. The early history of modernscience is based on the Aristotelian dualities of cause and effect — the logic of diacritic thinking.

Synesthetic thinking has been recognized for centuries but is often not considered valid. Synesthetic process can, however, be credited with recent developments in technology, and it is the basis for modern science and the field theory of nuclear particle physics. Spirituality and spiritual practice require a synesthetic perspective.

The synesthetic thought process occurs predominantly in the right side of the brain and serves as the basis for creative, innovative thinking. Although commonly associated with Einstein and field theory, synesthetic thinking has been described in the earliest writings of the history of humankind. It is this metaphoric, Big Picture thinking that results in communication that creatively ties together entities that at first appear unrelated.

Synesthetic thinking is often discounted as being imprecise. Our natural inclination is to group things into categories. We become anxious when they don't fit, because it requires us to adjust our thinking. We must either make an immediate change, or at least accept the inevitability of change at some future time.

Metaphors are not used in an attempt to be completely precise, but rather to stimulate new perceptions without a completely "rational" framework. They are, in a sense, "thinking bridges" between the apparently opposing forces of rationality and creativity. Metaphors can take us beyond our everyday awareness to a point where we can actually see our own lives from a different perspective.

The metaphoric process of balance thinking, as you will see, can enlarge your perceptions of your own life. Your reality can become more connected, more comprehensible and more internally consistent through the greater understanding that comes from metaphoric elaboration. The principles of Balance, therefore, can be found in poetry, songs, stories and drama. Indeed, they are present in any linguistic or creative activity, as well as in the aphorisms of everyday common sense. An understanding of these integrative principles can be as applied to an act as mundane as chopping wood or as transcendent as reading *Death of a Salesman*.

UNBALANCED DUALISTIC THINKING

Unbalanced, diacritic speech and thought patterns were typical of primitive people. Unbalanced perceptions result from easily observable, superficial assessments and may result in simplistic conclusions of cause and effect. Limited by black-and-white thinking, they are *exclusive* rather than *inclusive*. These conceptual patterns, passed down by our ancestors, made us believe we could change people just as easily as we might change a tire on a car. Categorical conceptual patterns describe content, not process. They emphasize either/or groupings of events and people in an effort to *explain* the changes in the natural order. Through these categorizations, our predecessors gained a sense of control.

Unbalanced language and coping patterns deal with the limited reality of things as they *appear to be at a given moment in time.* They are limited psychic perceptions due to defensive patterns of thinking. Diacritic language patterns are useful in helping us relate to the world of stop signs, one-way streets and speed limits. If we break one of these societal rules, we may get a ticket and, in so doing, will create problems for ourselves. Such observations are simple, obvious and useful when the world is consistent. But diacritic patterns of thought can leave us arrested in our development with small-minded perceptions.

Diacritic thought patterns are unable to fully describe the larger order, or the "field," in the order of relationships. Applied to relationships, they are reductionistic. They are limited to such superficial perceptions as "You're just like your mother," "You know how men are," or "You're trying to hurt me." At their worst, these are relationship *assumptions.* Often they are used as defensive interpretations. These simplistic thinking patterns can presume the worst and are often manipulative in intent. Guilt-provoking, diacritic remarks are reductionistic and cast in negative terms. Other reductionistic perceptions such as those found in "love" are simplistically positive. They spring from limited awareness of others and "rose-colored" preconceptions.

Diacritic patterns are ones of denial, gratification and comfort. We have been developing these dualistic patterns, which provide us with a sense of apparent safety, since the days of primitive humans, in an effort to protect ourselves from clearly seeing and accepting the larger and more natural Balanced Order.

Diacritic patterns resemble a broken record of self-talk. They perpetuate our fear of pain and change by rigidly defending us against the change that is inherent in our lives. They keep us locked in our paleolithic caves by using the mind to ward off perceptions of natural change in our effort to keep things as they appear to be. The dualistic mind makes us either too aloof or too helpless to cope with real change. It causes us to be out of balance and manipulative. Our limited, *unbalanced* reality is superimposed like a dream over the *balanced* reality that actually exists on a deeper level of awareness. Such short-term thinking uses the power of our minds, our language and our intellect to repeatedly differentiate, change, manipulate and, ultimately, *avoid* reality. Recovery is awakening from that dream.

Sometimes, we use the same techniques in an effort to manipulate, avoid, analyze or change the reality of our most personal relationships. We use dualistic thinking to form superficial, patterned responses to relationship difficulties, because we don't understand the usefulness of pain in our own self-development process. Dualistic communication is a primitive, caveman response compared with the more evolved Balance perceptions and behaviors that are available for our use.

The diacritic "language map" that we use clearly doesn't represent the real, naturally balanced territory of our lives, and the inaccurate maps in our minds don't lead us to the places we could be going. In truth, our lives have the potential to be much richer and fuller than our limited vision perceives them to be.

The following parable will give you another example of unbalanced thinking in action:

> Two monks, who had taken vows of chastity, were walking together. They came upon a beautiful woman who hesitated to cross a river. One monk picked her up, carried her across the water, and delivered her to the other side. The monks continued walking silently for several hours. Suddenly the one who had not carried the woman criticized his chivalrous companion.
>
> "You carried that woman across the river back there!" he said accusingly.
>
> "Yes," replied the other monk. "And you have carried her these many miles."

DEEP RECOVERY / 33

Can you see how the accuser was attached to dualistic thought? Using left-brain logic, he was stuck in black-and-white thinking and could see only the superficial, apparent order of things. He had tunnel vision. But, in truth, *his* emotions were more attached to the woman, the rules and the event than were those of his friend who had actually carried her.

The Balance Order is a process that goes beyond stop signs and speed limits. It transcends fixation, control and avoidance. Through Balance awareness, you can achieve a higher level of relationship self-management that will offer opportunities for less pain, fewer conflicts and greater leadership responsibility.

Balance awareness is naturally designed. While it transcends the obvious and mundane, it nevertheless includes those observations as useful and essential — as a part of the whole. The diacritic rules do apply most of the time, but you must eventually enlarge your thinking to the Balance process in order to successfully manage your life.

With the help of some ancient and contemporary metaphors and aphorisms, we will progress beyond the primitive, black-and-white perceptions that have taken us through our everyday lives thus far. The Balance patterns are recognizable in ancient writings from the earliest work of the Diamond Heart Sutra (written by Zen monks hundreds of years B.C.) and the Bible, to the Greek philosophers and Chinese warrior generals. Today, we can see them in our contemporary music and movies. They are available, but seemingly disconnected, from our dualistic awareness. By understanding these patterns, we can penetrate the superficial awareness of our diacritic language system.

Most often, we see balanced patterns operating when we see activities that prevent victimization of self or others. In a relationship, balanced communications show respect for the other person's perceptions and limitations. Such communications accept the differences and seek balance, rather than victory or recrimination. Balanced understanding perceives and accepts the transcendent, larger natural order that exists not only in the natural universe, but in our relationships, as well. Through practice, we will be able to contrast synesthetic, balanced thinking patterns with those defensive, diacritic approaches that are loaded with desire, great expectations and attachments.

By understanding the Balance Order, we will ultimately be freed of some of the pain in our relationships, and we'll be freed to pursue personal growth. With that new awareness, we can learn to recognize responsible behavior. We can also begin to recognize how relationships fit within the larger natural order in which all things have significance and are interrelated. Small relationship events can become important opportunities. Pain will become a useful teacher. Other difficult life events, that may have seemed significant in the past, will shrink in importance when held up against millennia and the universe.

As a bonus, you can have a lot of fun with Balance understanding, because balanced thinking provides opportunities for cosmic humor and for more frequently having a laugh at oneself.

The natural Big Picture of the complexity of relationships entails a broader, deeper field of issues and an order beyond the ordinary language and simple conceptualizations that we often use. The Balance way of relationships — the *process* of relationships — is not frozen in time. It includes many variables which are constantly undergoing change.

To fully understand how we find ourselves confused, we must not only understand how we *think* diacritically, but also how we *use language* diacritically.

In the next chapter, we will discuss specifically how the language we use can itself create problems as we attempt to solve our difficulties. If you use only a black-and-white, diacritic thought process or a reductionistic language base, you will not be able to conceptualize the deeper metaphors — the natural, connecting metaphors that exist in our relationships. And you will be controlled by your own limited awareness far more than you could ever be controlled by natural events.

Your everyday language and diacritic thought process tend to be used to stop change and to keep things locked up in time. We practice "time-binding," as Alfred Korzybski has pointed out, and lock ourselves conceptually into yesterday's ideas. When we bind events and people in time, we reduce the variables associated with change. We think reductionistically and, thereby, limit ourselves.

With awareness of your new Balance Order, you will realize that you are only as controlled as you perceive yourself to be. If you can see that your humanity, that your very existence, can and does fit into this larger, naturally changing order, you can free yourself for the productive use of your own life. Even more importantly, through the ongoing study and improvement of yourself and your relationships, you will ultimately serve the long-term benefit of those who follow.

3

Language And The Big Picture:

Your Words Can Trap You

*I saw myself on the central mountain of the world,
the highest place, and I had a vision because I was
seeing in the sacred manner of the world. But the
central mountain is everywhere.*
                              Black Elk,
                              Sioux Medicine Man

This life is full of lessons. It is full of opportunities to
learn and to see Black Elk's sacred vision. Each of us has
the capacity to stand on the central mountain. Each step,
each lesson and each difficulty should take us higher up
the mountain of seeing the Big Picture — the larger sacred
order and the Balance plan. Each step takes us away from
the patent simplicity of categorization that occurs with
only positive or negative thinking. Yet, under duress we
often seem to be at war with ourselves, our fellows and our
environment. Struggling against understanding, we take
action to avoid and control — ever trying to stick with
what we think we know.
    I once heard a story about a sly, old tobacco farmer and
his mule. It seems he had put his mule up for sale and
someone came to examine it. The wary buyer asked him
to hitch the mule up to a tobacco sled to see how the animal pulled. The farmer complied, and the mule took off

with the sled — down the hill, across the creek, up the hill on the other side and into the woods where he ran smack into a tree.

The buyer turned to farmer and said, "I do believe you're trying to sell me a blind mule."

The sly farmer quickly replied, "That mule ain't blind, son. He just don't give a damn."

An understanding of Balance patterns will keep us from running into the many trees we don't see, simply because we don't care to look. Many of us can't see because we're too busy seeking safety. We seek to be safe and protected within our own limited experience of reality. With blinders on, we run away and hide, because we don't understand how we learn or how reality can teach us.

Conversely, like the mule, others sometimes run blindly *ahead* with pride. *Hubris,* meaning pride, was the fundamental tragic element in the Greek theater tradition dating back more that 2,500 years ago. Pride continues to serve as a filter for reality. Our problems, as we shall soon see, are not new. They existed long before recorded history.

Unfortunately, we lack the sacred vision, the *awareness* of the larger Balance Order. This Order is coded. It's secret and sacred, beyond the grasp of everyday life, but easily available to anyone who is motivated to see further. Your capacity for observation of that Order will grow as you practice seeing in the sacred manner of Black Elk.

Charlotte Joko Beck, in her book *Everyday Zen,* drew an analogy to describe the progression of higher order vision. She pointed out that when you first start to practice Zen, it's similar to being caught in the middle of a busy intersection; there is no place to rest, and traffic is coming at you from everywhere. Rapid changes distract you. But, as you develop a more objective look, you can begin to see clear areas, and you may even reach the sidewalk. The sidewalk offers a different view. Later, as you advance further, you may be able to climb up and view the traffic from a third floor balcony. Climbing still higher, you eventually see from the top of a high building that the traffic forms patterns below. Up there, your view is larger, more inclu-

sive. Your objectivity and awareness will be more consistently operative, and you'll be less caught up in the tumult
of your life. You'll be in a place where you can regularly
pay attention.

The search for understanding must start with the basics
— at street level, so to speak. We have to examine the
noise and hubbub of our own language patterns, because
we humans are often confused by our own
communications.

LANGUAGE

If you think your problems started only with your
mother or father, think again. Our problems started, in
fact, about 400,000 years ago. It was then that we first
began to use fire and gather communally. It was then, pa-
leontologists believe, that *Homo erectus* became the first
pre-human being to speak. They suggest that before him,
Australopithicus screamed some pre-language warnings,
but with the arrival of *Homo erectus,* the voice box lowered
and primitive speech began.

It is through the evolution of speech and language that
we are able to pass on our perceptions, our "maps," of the
world. It is through the medium of communication that we
function as global animals, advanced in our ability to manage nature. Because of speech and language, we are not
isolated. Instead, we are a group — an extended family,
gathering around the communal fires from New York City
to Outer Mongolia.

There's no question that language has guided human intellectual and technological advancement. We are fortu-
nate in that we are able to learn from the experiences of
those who came before us.

> *"By means of symbols (language), man becomes
> free of situations and events in his learning pro-
> cess. Put otherwise, this means that it is not nec-
> essary to experience something in order to learn
> about it."*
>
> Leslie A. White,
> Linguist and Anthropologist

However, the symbols of language do have limits. Because they are only *symbols* and not, in fact, the things they represent, they are not reality. As Leslie White points out, the language symbols have "imperceptible values lodged in physical forms." Words may have many meanings which can vary for each listener and, consequently, can get us into serious trouble. On the other hand, the words themselves can carry fixed illusions and imagined perceptions that attempt to fix and stop an ever-changing world. Our problems begin with the way we experience the world through the communication process — through the use of language.

Speech advanced us as a race by setting up ways to avoid the direct experience of reality. Fewer people died because mastodon hunters could predict and communicate the movements of those prehistoric animals. Our homes, our heat, our skyscrapers and our medicines are all language-based means of coping with nature. We have, through language, managed (in some degree) to alter nature so that it serves our needs.

Peter Conserva, a veterinarian friend of mine, once shared with me an observation from his training. He said that animals are weakest in the part of their bodies where they are most highly bred and developed. Race horses most often break down in their legs, and dachshunds have difficulty with their backs. Cows most often have problems with their udders. And man, of course, has profound problems with his brain, the center of his language and perceptual abilities.

The observation that language can create problems isn't, of course, new. Dr. Edward deBono, an international lecturer on creativity and lateral thinking (a method for developing creative thought) has often made the observation that language is one of our greatest limitations. And Rudyard Kipling, in a speech given February 14, 1923, said, "Words are, of course, the most powerful drug used by mankind." The problem is that words, a mere representation of reality, often become our reality.

KORZYBSKI

It is Alfred Korzybski, founder of the field theory of general semantics, who spelled out the difficulty with language most completely. He pointed out that language is not only representational and reductionistic, but is also time-bound. To say, for example, that a particular man is "old," may descriptively restrict him to being categorized only by his chronological age and, in so doing, may completely overlook his energy, attitude and intellect. "Old" is a reductionistic categorization of a complex individual. To further complicate things, such a limited category as "old" becomes even more weighted and limited by the positive or negative connotations attached to that word. The connotations of the speaker imply values and negative or positive limitations to the listener.

We use language to fix things in time, to grasp and control them as they are that moment, and thereby eliminate some of the variables of change. Some aspects of language, such as poetry, go against that trend. Poetry is synesthetic, not diacritic. But ordinary speech, both oral and written, may serve to lock us in conceptually if we aren't appropriately aware of the potential problems with simple, often purely reductionistic thinking and expression. Through language, we can unconsciously lock ourselves and others into a "safe" structure that seeks to avoid or control the ongoing process of the change.

> *Language fails entirely to make one crucial distinction. It assumes that words and the things they describe are identical, and so fails to distinguish between "maps" in our minds and the territory such maps refer to. The words may, in fact, falsify the territory to which they refer.*
>
> *Charles Hampden-Turner,*
> *Psychologist*

Through limitations in our awareness, we can unconsciously lock ourselves in by time and symbol. Words may *reduce* the object to which they refer. For example, an

"Indian" may be an East Indian or a Native American. If he is a Native American, he may be an Apache, a Navaho or a Sioux. Even at that, the site of his origins doesn't begin to describe the totality of what and who he is. An Indian is more than "an Indian." Such a problem exists in the current misuse of the term "codependent." A person with codependency traits is more than simply a "codependent." Likewise, a person suffering from alcoholism is more than just an "alcoholic." In actuality, an alcoholic can also be codependent at the same time.

Words may also lock objects in time. Left in the sun over time, a red boat cushion will fade to pink. But at what specific moment does it stop being red and become pink? Over time, many things change completely. Unconsciously, our language patterns become a way in which we simplistically represent the world in which we live.

> *We create a map, or model, of the world which we use as a basis for our behavior. The model that we create to guide us through the world is based upon our experiences and what we've been told. Each of us may create a different model, and we each thus come to life in a somewhat different reality.*
>
> *Richard Bandler and*
> *John Grinder,*
> *Psycholinguists*

We each have different maps that represent reality as we see it, but may, in fact, inadequately represent the world as it actually is. As Korzybski said in his book *Science and Sanity* "A map is not the territory it represents, but, if correct, it has a similar structure to the territory, which accounts for its usefulness."

To be useful and practical, the meaning of the language must closely approximate the territory it represents. The ultimate efficiency and vitality of language can be regularly rediscovered in its everyday usefulness. Impractical, unbalanced ideas aren't able to be usefully shared because they provide inadequate, limited maps. Limited maps, those with reductionistic and simplistic positive or negative values or implications, take the user down paths of self-destruction and don't tell where the holes in the road are. Reductionistic, time-bound maps are dualistic and *create* oppositional thinking. Tripping on our own words, we fall all over our most treasured concepts. Indeed, we *victimize ourselves* through our use of prehistoric patterns in language.

From a "mental health" point of view, we might define our territory as Freudian, Jungian or Ericksonian. Each theory suggests a certain plan of how the therapist deals with the patient. But, recovery is about how we each deal with our individual experience of reality. From a recovery point of view, we can "believe" in codependency or discount it. If we accept the label, what do we do with it? Our lives are limited by our words and our concepts as we place unconscious values on them. Our opportunities for development are caught up in conceptual language traps.

Over time, however, language and concepts wear out their own usefulness. Whatever guidance one *Homo erectus* hunter gave another regarding mastodons has little significance now for the obvious reason that mastodons no longer exist. Or, as Alfred North Whitehead said, "The systematic thought of ancient writers is now nearly worthless, but their *detached* insights are priceless." The reason is that their synesthetic insights described *process,* while their systematic thought often described diacritic *content.* Indeed, our own formal, diacritic education is synesthetically recast by additional life experience. What we at first learn from the outside is recast by our integrated inside experience.

The important point is that limited thinking binds us in time to the thought patterns of our immediate predecessors and mentors, or even to those of early cavemen. So, it's important for our symbolic communication to carry the sort of feeling, tonality and worldliness that can prevent primitive, reductionistic thinking or labeling.

To put it another way, it's what we say *and* how we say it. Concepts change, words change and the natural universe changes. But, the Big Picture remains the same. If we try, through fear and defensiveness, to bind our concepts in time as if they are changeless, it becomes readily apparent to the enlightened listener. Yet many of us do just that as we struggle to hang on to concepts, biases and views from the past. We often cling to the false and limited perceptions of our mentors.

We all attempt to categorize and evaluate the many reality variables we encounter. For example, if I tell you that I am a physician, that has one category of meaning to you. If I tell you I'm a psychiatrist, it has another. And, if I say I lived in Dexter, Missouri, and went to Culver Military Academy, still other boxes and associations would spring to mind that might influence you to form a negative or positive judgment of me as a person. You may subconsciously place each statement into a category that is limited by time and space, positive or negative attributes.

None of these facts about myself implies anything about my values, my capacity for leadership or my tenacity. But you may have, nevertheless, formed certain preconceived notions about me based upon those simple statements. You will likely associate them to your previous experience with physicians, psychiatrists, people from Missouri or military school graduates and, based upon your experience, will categorically reduce them and place those simplistic positive or negative qualities upon them.

Being aware of the problems and limitations in our language is a complicated, but important, first step in understanding what is said in this book. Today, we are in an interesting time of new conceptual developments — of new terms like "addiction" and "codependency." And yet we are still, in a sense, a primitive people locked in by preconceptions and huddled safely behind an edifice of brick words.

We take our magic words and run with them. Words such as "black," "woman," " Catholic," " child," " addict," or "male," are all examples of constructs that pigeonhole us and limit our expression and development. Why? Because we hear them as finite. Because we accept the limited territories of word symbols, and because the words create an element of safety.

Such a phenomenon has occurred, in some respects, with the word "codependent," known in some critical circles as that "C" word (we'll discuss codependency in more depth later). Over time, the subgroups we have tagged with the term "codependent" will, in fact, change. Our collective understanding of these subgroups has already changed dramatically in the past ten years. Our strength is that we are able to categorize. Our weakness is that we think categorically in "100-percent" terms. We permit our strength to trap us.

I have often seen this phenomenon of categorical, reductionistic thinking in my work with alcoholics and drug addicts who, many forget, are people. They have a problem, but they're still human beings. After all, they are not 100-percent alcoholic anymore than a codependent is 100-percent codependent. Likewise, a corporate executive isn't totally (100-percent) an executive, and evangelist Jim Bakker wasn't 100-percent spiritually motivated.

Can you see how, through words, we try to cut the world into clear, black-and-white groupings that are bound in time by the limitations of our perceptions and knowledge. A person who recognizes and admits he or she has a 10-percent "codependency problem" can quickly become 100-percent codependent through language. Language can freeze thought, bind creativity and lock us into the past or the future. Whatever else we are as human beings may be neglected and minimized if we define ourselves so reductionistically in a single word.

This locked-in, primitive way of using language limits us in other ways, as well. There are two ways, for example, in which we learn. First, we learn through our own experience and second, from others (parents, teachers, books, etc.). We are sometimes taught through language to *avoid* real experience which may be perceived by others as painful and apparently of little use.

A parent may, for example, tell a child that whites (blacks, Mexicans, etc.) are not to be trusted and to avoid them. It would take years for that child to learn that trust is not an issue of race. The parent's reductionistic comment keeps the disconnection alive and places the child in a *passive* role within his own decision-making process.

In other instances, a parent might refuse appropriate teaching opportunities and instead *push* the child into premature *active* experience without the necessary training in the process of life. A child raised on such statements as, "You're smart, do it yourself," may feel stupid and perplexed or overconfident. They are taught swimming by being thrown off the dock. Regardless of the outcome, they feel disconnected from others and experience difficulties as a result of their subsequent defensive posturing. They can become defensive through action or defensive through passivity. Through unbalanced training patterns, we can become either *language-dependent* (hoping to solve our problems by talk) or *action-dependent* (feeling that the language process is useless).

The major problem with the defensive use of language is the fact that we can, through talk or thought, avoid risk and think we have grown. We often become overeducated and undertrained — educated, that is, in concepts and undertrained in reality. Thus, we have created the cliché about college professors being locked in ivory towers without any experience in the real world. Some reportedly have advanced degrees but can't open the hood of the car. Their focus is limited to intellectual growth as they avoid everyday realities.

But, there is hope. Most of us, consciously or not, are seeking balance. Evolved thinking and integrated creative opportunities *are* available to us and can be demonstrated at every interface with reality. We can choose to be comprehensive in our approach to life, or we can choose to limit ourselves to the family, the office and perhaps the club. Our everyday relationships require balanced action, balanced language and communication. Evolved language can change our "self-talk" inner world — our view of ourselves, our self-esteem, our confidence, our values and our relationships. It can reduce our self-imposed limitations.

By recognizing that the root of our problems rests in *how* we think and communicate, we can begin to understand why words oftentimes can't solve them. It's indeed true that if the world is presented to us in neat language bundles, and we aren't entirely *aware* of that packaging process, then we might, in fact, find ourselves spending our lives simply sorting those language bundles. Yes, it is possible to sort aspects of reality through language, rather than to risk experiencing it. But as Korzybski pointed out, this is clearly not the high road to self-development. It is, rather, only a path to illusion. And through this system of illusion, we can, with our own time-bound language system, talk ourselves into "failure" or "expertise." And in the process, we miss out on what our own real life experience with relationships could teach us about ourselves.

REALITY

Our most important lessons in life come from our own personal experience with the real world. Interestingly, the physical world outside appears relatively fixed and unchanging. We can see that we are able to avoid aspects of it by organizing ourselves — building skyscrapers, installing air conditioning and so on. It *appears* that we have fixed the changes of nature. But the truth, as we know from nuclear particle physics, is that even the apparently fixed world is constantly undergoing change. Heraclitus said it so eloquently in the sixth century B.C.: "You cannot step twice into the same river for other waters are continually flowing on." A contemporary rock group, the Eagles, put it another way: "We may lose and we may win, though we will never be here again." Over time, everything in nature changes. Over time, the natural order for human beings *is* change.

One reason that we often find ourselves uncomfortable with change is that it takes time and energy to separate our fixed perceptions and expectations from the *reality* of the thing or the event that has changed. Reality, as defined here, refers to the way *things actually are* at a given moment — *not* necessarily as you *perceive them to be* or have perceived them to be in the past.

As you can see, reality is not time-bound. To repeat, reality is the state of things as they are now, rather than the way they were at some previous time in your life, the way they were in your parents' lives or how they might be in the future. But, since we are insecure about what change will bring, we allow our *perceptions* to cloud or change the reality so that it fits with our patterns of comfort. Most changes that occurred during primitive times were life-threatening, and our early ancestors resisted them. So, down through the ages, we have developed as a race of animals by "fixing" natural change or attempting to prevent it from happening. Today, we are still using our minds to ward off the cycles of nature. But in so doing, we also ward off the opportunity for reality lessons.

Some reality we can change, and some we can't. We can change a tire, make a bed or wash the dishes. But, we can't change the past — what has already happened. We can't do it over, because it isn't the same river. *The only thing we can change is our perception of what happened.* And with that new perception and the new eyes we have developed, we will mature over time. We can remember the past — use it and learn from it — but we can't change the events or people involved. *We can't change the past, but the past can change us.* And our most difficult traumas serve as reminders that we aren't as much in control as we think we are.

There are, actually, two kinds of reality, both of which change constantly over time: 1) The reality of the external world and 2) our internal reality (our perceptions). And if, because of limited vision, we don't keep up with the changes of either reality, we become locked in, fixed, reductionistic and time-bound in our own development. We remain primitive. The trauma and pain keep us fixed and focused on the outside, the inside, or both. Because we can change *some* things, we become frustrated with the recognition of our inability to change *all* things. Can you see this as another example of categorical thinking?

Psychoanalyst Ernst Becker, in the *Denial of Death*, correctly observes that we are awash with lies and illusion:

> We don't want to admit that we are fundamentally dishonest about reality, that we do not really control our own lives. We don't want to admit that we do not stand alone (that we are

dependent), that we always rely on something that transcends us, some system of ideas and powers in which we are embedded and which support us. This power is not always obvious ... it can be a person, a goal, an activity, a passion, a dedication to a game, a way of life that like a comfortable web keeps a person buoyed up and ignorant of himself, of the fact that he does not rest on his own center.

The defenses that form a person's character support a grand illusion, and when we grasp this we can understand the full driveness of man. He is driven away from himself, from self-knowledge, self-reflection. He is driven toward things that support the lie of his character, his automatic equanimity. But he is also drawn precisely toward those things that make him anxious, as a way of skirting them masterfully, testing himself against them, controlling them by defying them. We enter into *symbiotic relationships* in order to get the security we need, in order to get relief from our anxieties, our aloneness and our helplessness; but these relationships bind us, they enslave us even further because they support the lie we have fashioned. It is fateful and ironic how the *relationship lie* we need in order to live dooms us to a life that is never really ours.

Even with the inevitable reality of death, the ultimate separation from our loved ones, we use mental tricks that protect us emotionally. We fear the reality of the *change,* positive or negative. It doesn't matter if the change is from the death of a loved one or career success. We deny that fear of change. We doom ourselves to a life that is never really ours. And as a result, we form attachments and dependencies, through language, that create even more pain than the original pain of the natural order. We retreat from reality and change (i.e. growth) to stasis, forming dependencies and any kind of attachment that will temporarily shelter us from the anxiety of the next moment. Relationships and drugs are only two of the many attachments that people use to avoid reality. But in the end, we are alone with our own experience.

Any pattern or word that keeps us from the Balance Order, that keeps us locked in diacritic, limited thinking, will bring us pain. Our attachments and dependencies build upon one another and gradually keep us from knowing our true selves. They keep us from the opportunities that exist in our own lives — locked in a life of illusions and dreams.

Automatic, dreamlike alteration or manipulation of your personal relationship reality prohibits or postpones the lessons you must learn. The longer the lessons are put off, the harder and more difficult they are to accept and understand, and the more you are doomed to reenact the pain. You must accept your reality, experience it and grow from it, rather than simply manipulate it through concepts and language. Otherwise, you will pay the ever-increasing price of emotional pain.

Our desire for comfort, our reductionistic communication process, and our understanding of psychology have unintentionally lead some of us to entertain the illusion that we can be permanently fixed and safe. We believe that if only we can avoid certain things, we will be secure. Yet ironically, we are often faced with the very problems we seek to avoid. If we seek solitude, we find ourselves interrupted. If we seek companionship, we find ourselves rejected.

Over time, we are repeatedly challenged by an odd *Rule of Paradox:* What we want eludes us, and we often don't want what we have. Or, in the words of an adage, "The grass is often greener on the other side of the fence." We wish for a different reality. We don't know how to use the reality we have.

Similarly, things that are usually perceived as assets (beauty, brains, money, power) can, over time, often become liabilities in that they may encourage the avoidance of reality. On the other hand, circumstances in life that are generally perceived as liabilities (poverty, trauma, addiction or dependency problems) may, in fact, paradoxically become assets if they can be accepted as useful lessons. The opposites are connected. Balance goes beyond boxes.

It is paradoxical, but true, that difficulties can change our perceptions and encourage a clearer view of the higher order. The balanced, natural order of change tugs at our desire to remain fixed, and we find ourselves regularly confronted with what we seek to avoid.

Understanding the process of change is imperative in balanced relationships. As we grow away from our programmed childhood experiences, we develop new ways of seeing the world. We change our views and our perspective. If, for example, your mother didn't like Southerners and you find yourself living in the South, you will have to change. If, on the other hand, you avoid moving South because of your childhood programming, you are indeed limited. Tragically, some people go to the extreme of killing themselves because they fear new reality — they can't face leaving home. Others simply stay home, stay stuck and bore themselves to death.

Bill Gove, a professional speaker, tells this interesting story about perceptions: Three men sat at a table: One from the Bronx, one from Tampa and one from the Everglades. Someone threw a king snake on the table in front of each man. The terrified fellow from the Bronx ejected from his seat with projectile force and fled from the room. The man from Tampa merely brushed the snake to the side, much as one would a bothersome fly. The man from the Everglades picked the snake up, studied it for a moment, and stuck it in his pocket so that he could take it home to kill rats in the barn.

The same reality — the same snake — existed for all three men. But each man had different perceptions and different programming. The man from the Bronx thought in primitive, reductionistic terms. His mind registered only the word "SNAKE!" and all the negative connotations commonly associated with the word. The man from Tampa knew it was harmless but saw no value in it. At the other extreme, the man from the Everglades perceived the snake as useful. They each focused on different, *incomplete* characteristics of the same snake. As we gain the larger order view, we can begin to see the *whole* picture for ourselves, instead of the partial picture we have been programmed to perceive.

The mechanism of denial is a primitive mental tool that moves us away from reality. So potent is this internal defense that it may even convince serious drug addicts that they have no problem. Sometimes, denial may work selectively on aspects of a certain issue. In relationships, we see it all the time: He is a 15-percent friendly and courteous fellow, but an 85-percent alcoholic, womanizer and dishonest person. His wife, who is frightened of being alone, denies the 85-percent. She doesn't want to see that unhealthy part of her partner. And, *temporarily,* the denial succeeds in avoiding the painful relationship reality.

In another example, an employer is unhappy with an employee who has made a mistake that might be a one-time, 10-percent item. This same employee is a 90-percent hard-working, honest, caring individual who, over time, has contributed well to the company. Nevertheless, the negative, judgmental employer fires the employee for his lack of perfection. Angry, the employer artificially exaggerates the 10-percent problem and denies the 90-percent positive qualities of the person.

Denial shields us from those things that our inadequacies or fear can't bear to face. *It keeps the observer apparently safe.* We don't have to deal with the whole person. Instead, we can focus only on the good or bad, depending on how it suits our purposes. In that manner, people might say something such as, "He's worthless," or "She's perfect." But, such observations are reductionistic, limiting and certainly not in tune with the sacred higher order. Such thoughts and remarks are primitive, *Homo erectus* categorical thoughts, and they are uncharacteristic of Big Picture thinkers.

PAIN

The Big Picture is not complete without discussing the importance of pain in our lives. Anyone setting out on a journey of self-discovery must understand the usefulness of pain. Now, that's not to say that you should seek pain out, but that you can learn to use it for personal growth. Pain serves as a reminder that you aren't thinking of the larger order of things, and it can bring understanding through a renewed awareness of the lesson process.

When we experience emotional pain, we are likely to react with shocked and indignant thoughts such as, "This shouldn't be happening," "Why me?" or "What did I do to deserve this?" Intellectually, we know about change, but we refuse to accept it emotionally. Reality brings frightened attachment patterns. Attachments bring pain. We feel the pain, but we don't know how to use it.

Human beings experience three different kinds of pain. Each of the three has a common factor in that the person experiencing the pain cannot control or change the reality of the situation.

1. *Natural Pain.* Otherwise known as fate. This is pain caused by natural events. Imagine, for example, you are out playing golf. The forecast has called for a bright, sunny day with balmy breezes. Suddenly, halfway through the course, the clouds break open and you get drenched. Aggravating? Sure. But, you have to deal with this natural event, because it simply cannot be controlled.

Another example can be witnessed in any airport. I saw it often myself, as I flew back and forth between Norfolk and Philadelphia during my psychoanalytic training. In the winter, the Norfolk airport occasionally would be fogged in. Standing at the Philadelphia flight gate, it was interesting to see the passengers who went into orbit because there was fog in Norfolk. The reason for their rage was that they were unable to *control* a natural event. They wanted *power* over the fog. They thought they should be able to *demand* a change in the fog's location. They wanted to *kill* the messenger at the gate. Natural pain is caused by what you think *shouldn't* happen to you.

2. *Conscious Self-Victimization.* This type of pain occurs when people walk into a problematic work or personal relationship reality with both eyes open — rec-

ognizing that they are likely to get hurt. They consciously feel they can handle it. Yet, once they try, it becomes more painful or difficult than they thought, and they experience pain. It's like walking out into the rain. You know you are going to get wet, but you don't realize just how uncomfortable the chill and wetness will be until you experience it. I was recently treating a woman who, though very young, was into her third marriage to an alcoholic. Without meaning to be funny, she told me that she believed she'd had enough practice with the first two husbands and that *she would be able to change this one.* She knew she was in trouble. She could see it coming even before she married the guy. Her mistake was in feeling powerful enough to change the reality of *his* chemical dependency. She saw his problems but used denial to minimize their impact on her life. And ultimately, she was hospitalized because of the depression that resulted when she couldn't change him.

3. *Unconscious Self-Victimization.* In this process, people are not conscious of the relationship patterns present in their lives that set them up for self-victimization. They believe that they understand the situation thoroughly and that they are doing quite well. They honestly don't see any problems at all. They unconsciously wear blinders which, ultimately, place them in a victim position. They walk into trees.

Most of us have unconscious relationship patterns that constantly recreate victim roles. The tyrannical boss, powerful and beyond reproach, will ultimately paint himself into a corner. He *thinks* he can control and change *all* things. He *thinks* he doesn't have a problem.

It is interesting that only one of the three ways in which we experience pain is through events that are *completely* out of our control. In the latter two types, events *would* be manageable, if only we had the internal strength and perceptual awareness to protect ourselves from submitting to the painful reality circumstances of our own relationship self-victimization. Two of the three ways we experience pain are, in fact, self-inflicted through our own thinking disorders.

All three types of pain are associated with a non-acceptance of the Balance Order. We set ourselves up through our own denial, our own illusion system and our own time-bound, locked-in patterns. We are unable to keep up with our own changing personal reality. We ask for the pain. But, in the end and regardless of the cause, we must be accountable to ourselves. That accountability brings opportunities and hope. It is through understanding our own limited thinking and the larger Balance Order that we can prevent the relentless self-victimization that haunts many of us through our lives. Through this new awareness, the unconscious patterns can become conscious, and we can assume full responsibility for our own problems.

BEGINNER'S MIND

"In the beginner's mind there are many possibilities, but in the expert's there are few."
Shunryu Suzuki,
Zen Philosopher

As you begin your travels through these pages and through each next moment, remember Suzuki's remarks. Open your mind. This book is not intended to make you an expert on anything. At best, it will make you a beginner. If you make the effort to see the Big Picture, you will soon see that experts are often fixed to words and concepts — to the way things used to be.

One recent definition of an expert is "one who knows more and more about less and less, until finally he knows absolutely everything about nothing." To be an expert is to be caught in the diacritic trap, stuck in time and place.

The words and concepts in this book will help you with the process of your life's relationships. I will even suggest some specific things for you to say on certain occasions. But isolated examples of technique do not lead to mastery. Words and technique without practice are only an illusion. Illusion is "pretend" activity. It is only through persistent practice and living your own relationships more fully that you can bring yourself closer to living in reality with the natural higher order. There is no such thing as perfection, although there are principles and correct actions. But, if you begin to feel that you're an expert or that you're "good," look out — get ready to be blind-sided or cold-cocked. Keep your hands up and your head down. This book can't keep you from getting hit. Contact with relationship reality is unavoidable in order to grow. *Deep Recovery* can only help you avoid *asking* for it.

While there is no such thing as relationship "perfection," there are also no relationship "mistakes." Each problem you face, each difficulty into which you place yourself and each relationship reality gives you the opportunity to see the Big Picture higher order beyond words and concepts. Each bump along the way gives you a chance to regroup your thoughts and skills of observation slightly higher up the central mountain than you were before. And the higher you go, the more you can see. You'll be able to understand yourself, your partners and your extended human family. Your view will show you the importance of values and discipline.

Your progression will come down to a matter of attitude. There is no safety in a categorical, patterned position. If you are determined to see life as adversarial, difficult and painful, then you will miss the higher order. If you are glib, cocky and think life's a piece of cake, get ready for a lesson. It will only be a matter of time until you take a hit. So, since time is all you have, why not use it to contribute to your Big Picture thinking — your larger order consciousness?

I once saw a cab driver wearing a large message button on his shirt. That button eloquently summarized the futility we often feel:

> This life is a test. It's only a test. If it was not a test, you would have received better instructions on where to go and what to do.

This book responds to that remark. It contains answers on where to go and what to do on a different level, so that life can be more meaningful than a simple exercise in guesswork.

The next chapter describes specific patterned behaviors. Remember — relationship problems *are* opportunities. The patterns that you discover will give you opportunities for self-awareness.

You *can* recognize how relationships actually fit together, and you *can* learn something from your own difficult life experiences. Through that understanding, you will feel less pain and, ultimately, you will find yourself quietly sharing the Big Picture message with others.

> *As you walk, you cut open and create that river bed into which the stream of your descendants shall enter and flow.*
> *Nikos Kazantzakis,*
> *Greek Poet*

4

The Illusion of Safety:

Your Patterns of Relationship Stuckness

"The Mind is its own place, and in itself can make a heaven of hell or a hell of heaven."
John Milton

Our language, our thoughts and our behaviors are too frequently defensive and unbalanced. Our comforts, our reductionistic preconceptions about others, our psychology and our educational system are arranged to prevent pain. As we begin to understand different aspects of reality, we try to codify them, pigeonhole them and avoid them. Our attitudes about ourselves and others limit our responses.

In the past, we humans worked in balance with the realities of changing nature. Our ancestors, such as the Native American Indians, saw all things as connected, and maintained respect for the natural balanced order of the environment.

Yet, we have become disconnected, unbalanced and lost. We have become drunk with consumption and avoidance. Defensiveness and comfort have become such obsessions that, on the larger scale, our species could literally destroy itself with nuclear "defensiveness." Our national and international difficulties are grand, extended examples of each individual's potential lack of balance. To the degree that our society is out of balance, we risk deterioration, disharmony, crime and war.

MAINTENANCE

As individuals, we often become users of people and things. Our society is, at its worst, comfort-driven — drawn to that which is disposable or expendable. Thus, we have our high divorce rates which parallel our extravagant use of Styrofoam cups and fast-food containers. The truth is that we discard people and things, rather than connect with them through personal action, effort and risk. Social scientist Lewis Mumford recognized our consumptive patterns several years ago and suggested an alternative in *The Pentagon of Power:* "Show me the *records of maintenance* and I'll show you the nation that will survive."

In a similar vein, many of us throw away developmental opportunities in our lives and relationships. *We discard these opportunities because we don't have the specific tools needed for maintenance.* Because we don't know how to use our painful experiences constructively, we run away from them.

Too often, we are not at peace with ourselves or our environment. We obsess about the past and worry about the future. We simply don't know what to do with our lives or how to develop our *self.* Psychology is difficult to understand with its mysterious myriad of abstractions ranging from oedipal fixations, to positive reinforcement, to codependency. And many of the self-help books are so focused and polarized, that it's difficult to integrate them into the larger order understanding. They often codify symptoms but offer no integrated action plan for ongoing recovery.

You may have decided, by this point, that you would like to start work on your beginner's mind attitude. You may also recognize that, in one sense, you're starting over each minute of your life anyway. Beginner's mind is an excellent basic maintenance attitude.

This chapter will show you specifically how to begin work on your own self-maintenance — your best self-protection and the foundation of self-management.

But first, you must get beyond thinking that self-management requires too much time or effort. You probably treat yourself much like you treat your car. You just want to fix whatever is broken and be done with it. Yet, the reason you keep getting broken in the first place is that you don't understand how you "work" or what to do for maintenance. You don't know how to "check your oil" — how to measure your inside experience.

Our self-neglect isn't a matter of laziness. We simply have too much to do and too many distracting reality variables. On the one hand, we have too many interesting, pleasurable experiences. On the other, there are too many fears and too much change. We are overwhelmed with goals, hurts, relationships, and television. It's all too confusing for us to think and act on our own behalf. In reaction to the disparity between what's going on inside ourselves and what's going on outside, we lose our focus. We become confused about our perceptions and use emotionally based defenses, such as denial, to protect ourselves against changing reality.

Behaviorally, we act to decrease the variables and to avoid the Big Picture. Remember that we avoid by thinking rather than doing. We also avoid by talking, and we avoid by using time-bound, dualistic black-and-white language. Does all of this seem too abstract? Than let's go back 400,000 years to *Homo erectus* and the beginnings of language.

Imagine, if you will, two cavemen wandering around the Transvaal several ice ages ago, in search of a mastodon. Suddenly, one hunter turns to the other and gives the primordial grunt for "Mastodon!" His partner hears the grunt and stops dead in his tracks, just in time to avoid being trampled by the animal he hadn't seen. That simple story demonstrates both the historical benefit and potential liability of language. The listening hunter survived, but he owed the speaker his life. There was, in fact, a bond formed between them at that moment. One man reduced the variables for the other by warning him of the reality of the approaching mastodon. But the listener, in turn, became obligated.

The communication language system we have developed creates a potential dependent-relationship problem. Its very nature encourages a debtor mentality. Out of a single grunt and a single response came the potential for dependency, debt and obligation between the cavemen. Because that one life-saving perception of reality was correct, the listener could have quickly overvalued other communicated perceptions that followed. He may have subsequently empowered the teacher and neglected to perceive and learn the reality lesson for himself. Their relationship could have evolved into a pattern, a method of safety and of avoidance of the mastodon. Or, the relationship pattern could have itself become the lesson. Their focus may have remained on the outside lesson of avoiding the mastodon instead of on the valuable inside relationship lesson that was present. From a process point of view, the mastodon was handled. But, the relationship changed. In handling the reality of the mastodon, the listener may have subtly shifted away from balanced self-maintenance by prioritizing or overvaluing his partner's subsequent observations.

If we are aware of these shifting relationship patterns, we will be more successful in our self-maintenance. It is in the dance of our relationships that we can come to see ourselves and our limitations. It is in the way we relate to our fellow humans that we can see how we're handling ourselves — how we're maintaining our lives. Our repetitive, dependent relationship patterns are the frontiers of the reality we haven't yet conquered and of the nature we haven't yet known. Our frozen relationship patterns create our most puzzling and painful attachments and protect us from actually seeing ourselves as we are. They ultimately create our pain.

Think about it. Emotional pain does not come from outside objects unless they have been anthropomorphized to some degree. Pain comes from our emotion-laden interactions with others. The roots of that pain reside in the assumptions that we will be properly cared for, that we won't be rejected, and that our friends and family will know enough to shout "mastodon!" Through the advent of language and our prolonged childhood dependency upon parental knowledge, we have developed two fundamental assumptions, or expectations, that lead us all astray. These expectations are based upon a desire to (1) prolong our childhood, and (2) decrease the reality variables with which we must cope.

The first fundamental expectation is that *some of us will reduce the variables for others by actively protecting them from reality through our language and/or action.* The tribe (society) expects that the caretakers will know, see and shout "mastodon!" for the tribe. So these warrior-heroes evolve as caretakers and keep the *outside* world at bay. Their expectation is to handle the outside world through protective caretaking action while *avoiding* the "unnecessary" variable of feeling. These warrior-heroes, traditionally males, deal with other tribes, animals, nature, etc. They reduce the variables they must face by not dealing with personal relationships or feelings. Because of their sacrifices, they feel entitled to special care and treatment back home. These leaders gain credibility by caring for others.

The second fundamental expectation is that *some of us will reduce our variables by having others protect us from the outside world.* This group tries to remain safe by keeping the fires burning and by caring for the children. They want others to shout "mastodon," and to point the way. They wish to be taken care of. They are child-caretakers, but otherwise are caretakees. Wanting someone else to manage the outside world, this group has focused for thousands of years on human relationships. They keep the kids in the cave, talk about their stomach aches, ask how they feel and caretake through verbalization and feeling. These child-keepers, traditionally women, cope by having others deal with the outside world. They are like children to their warrior-hero caretakers. Through their sacrificial caretaking activities, they feel entitled to special care and treatment at home. They are feeling and relationship-focused.

This prehistoric management of reality with specific role definition was practical then because it did reduce the reality variables. Men could focus on mastodons and women could focus on children. We have, for eons, been caught between two choices, the caretaker and caretakee. We are still often lost in these automatic relationships. Without language, we would all have the same role assignments: Hunt — Eat — Die. We humans use our language adaptively to prioritize our use of time and arrange the world. We can spend a lifetime on one job description. And when we form locked-in, frozen priority patterns, we become off balance. We keep arranging our world the same way even though external circumstances of change argue against that arrangement. We keep repeating the same activities in our relationships, even though they simply don't work.

Our abilities with language have allowed us to subspecialize in our relationships and assign ourselves separate duties. So it is that one does the dishes while the other cooks. And we frequently struggle to continue these arrangements even when the other person or the circumstances of life change. Our relationship patterns often keep us from dealing with our fellow humans in a respectful manner, because we want things our way. We don't want *change*.

In our investigation and study of nature, we have slowly learned that, in truth, we have little control. Because we can't order the rain to stop, it's our responsibility to go inside. Yet we continue to feel that we can control our *relationships*. Because we have brief moments of control over others through love, idealization, magical words, etc., we feel that we can consistently *control* them.

Regarding nature, we have grown to understand our own limitations relative to natural change. We know we must make adjustments to protect ourselves. But in relationships, we have developed little appreciation for our own patterns, our own preconceptions and our own limitations. We don't understand how to balance ourselves in relationship situations. We don't understand respectful self-protection.

Our relationships are as real as any natural reality. Each person is as a star or a tree — a discrete natural entity. But our user mentality, our non-maintenance thinking, sets us up to use relationships for our own satisfaction, just as we do other natural resources. And while we have learned to measure subatomic quarks in miles-deep Italian caves, from stars thousands of years dead, we are still primitive as cavemen in negotiating our relationships. Our knowledge of quarks may attest to our skills at measurement of the outside world, but our wars, our murder rate and our addiction epidemic demonstrate our confusion in relationship realities. We still find ourselves coping in primitive, stereotyped, patterned and defensive subspecialty roles that long ago lost their original significance or practical application.

We use our minds to escape from or distort relationship realities so that they fit into comfortable patterns. We avoid reality, not only with our loved ones, but also in our business, political and social lives. Through this avoidance, this Big-Picture blindness, we relentlessly victimize ourselves. Because we can't see our fellow humans in their natural context, we set *ourselves* up. Both our bedroom and boardroom relationships offer the illusion of safety. Both offer many illusion opportunities for the caretaker-caretakee dyad. We search for identity in either/or.

In trying to manage our personal reality and reduce our variables, we repeatedly find ourselves out of balance. Practicing either avoidance or control, we get locked into safety patterns of coping that are only illusions of protection. Though we may take satisfaction and comfort in our temporary protection from outside natural events, we must still cope daily with one remaining natural reality — our human partners. But take heart, because through them, we can find ourselves.

In the process of "managing" our relationships, we often use one of two deceptively simple coping patterns. These patterns are designed to reduce certain reality variables that some prefer not to address. But, they also warp the reality of perceptions and responsibilities in our relationships and eventually lead to self-victimization and emotional pain. These patterns are often unconscious, are fed by denial, and keep us from becoming fully integrated as human beings. They are repetitive, relatively fixed, and amazingly universal in their appearance. Based on dualistic, reductionistic thinking, these patterns keep us out of balance.

These two patterns can be recognized through the metaphor of the Lone Ranger and the Helpless Victim.

THE LONE RANGER

"Cowboys are special with their own brand of misery, from being alone too long ... Sadly in search of, and one step in back of, themselves and their slow moving dreams."
Willie Nelson
Country Singer

If you are old enough to remember, return with me to the thrilling days of yesteryear. Even today, I can see the masked man and his faithful Indian companion gallop across the black and white screen of my memories. As a child, my most valued possessions were two pearl-handled, silver six guns and their matching holsters. And as many of you probably did, I spent many hours in Lone Ranger practice.

Here's a trivia question. Do you remember how Clayton Moore became the silent masked avenger of the West? He was riding with his Texas Ranger friends in Box Canyon, when they were ambushed by the Butch Cavendish gang. All the Rangers were killed except one. Nursed back to health by a kind Indian who happened belatedly upon the scene, the surviving Ranger swore revenge on all those who were lawless in the West. With a mask, a white horse, silver bullets and a serious gray spandex suit, he became the Lone Ranger.

Think about the personal relationship characteristics of the Lone Ranger. Did he greet people warmly? Did he say goodbye? Did he have a wife and family? Did he want a ranch or retirement? Did he talk much? In short, did he connect in his personal relationships? No.

The Lone Ranger was a metaphor for the prototypical warrior-hero. He *reduced the reality variables* in his life by reducing the emphasis on personal relationships — on feelings and verbalization. He *avoided* relationships and worked on *controlling* external natural reality. He shoved his internal life, his feelings, inside. He didn't hate women or children. He was drawn to a higher order principle outside of himself — survival. So, he took on the task of caretaker and values-enforcer for the entire West. His favorite rationalization was that somebody had to do it.

The Lone Ranger served the West well, but as far as relationships went, he was out of balance. Focused on external reality, he could not cope with the potential pain of personal intimacy. Deep inside, he was vulnerable, but he hid it. Losing all of his best friends as he had, it was too hard to risk caring again. He was in pain. He hurt. And he was angry at those who attacked him. His life was a continual and repetitive vindication of a traumatic event. To master the trauma of being caught in an unpredictable, passive situation and almost killed, he became actively offensive. The reality of that surprise ambush hurt him. He was unprepared. He took a hard kendo swat across the chest. The pain burned in him relentlessly until he rode off in the dust of the final episode.

The Lone Ranger was out of balance because he felt victimized by reality. He began his quest in a victim role but vowed never to be victimized again. His reticence belied his sensitivity. He came out of the incident prepared. He was, in fact, defensively overprepared. He was hurt and swore never to be hurt again. But ultimately, he hurt himself by being alone — by having only one friend, no family, no home fire at the ranch and no warm bed. With his caretaker vow, he painted himself into a corner of vulnerability that showed in his disconnected, isolated safety net of diminished relationships. He victimized himself by avoiding the variables that relationships inevitably encourage — feelings, discussions, intimacy, commitment, and vulnerability.

A more contemporary figure who played the same role was Robert Redford in *Out of Africa*. He read poetry but

told little about himself. He was telepathically connected
to his companion, a Massi warrior. He couldn't say goodbye. Strong on the outside, he hid his tenderness on the
inside and felt misunderstood. Sadly, there are many of
these gun slingers who think the enemy is only "out
there." They can't see the potential danger within themselves. They deny the loneliness.

The following list describes the unbalanced characteristics of the seriously polarized and defensive Lone Ranger.
Do you know anyone like this?

1. *Avoids* relationship reality.
2. Tries to *control* external reality.
3. Often disrespects others and excessively respects
   self.
4. Denies vulnerability and, therefore, resists fear and
   sadness.
5. Favorite affect is anger. Favorite attitude is pride.
6. Non-verbal about themselves.
7. Cognitive and logical.
8. Displays non-existent or reduced emotions (wears a
   mask).
9. Reacts to outside stimuli in the following sequence:
   think, act and (maybe) feel much later. Sometimes
   reacts: think, think, think and maybe act.
10. Too strong on boundaries.
11. Action-oriented; believes actions speak louder than
    words.
12. Needs a go-fer such as Tonto, Sancho Panza, Gaby
    Hayes or Chester.
13. Expert sub-specialists who are inflexible, rigid and
    fixed. Thinking is biased, and values tend to be per-
    sonal, needs-driven and situationally determined.
14. Compulsive caretakers to themselves or others.
15. Angry when others don't agree with them. Anger
    covers fear.
16. Vain in appearance — constantly grooming.
17. Blames others. "I don't have a problem, you do."
18. Categorical (100%) thinker.
19. Strives for perfection. Struggles for control.
20. Covers mistakes for self or team.

21. Typical political belief: Cast out or kill the imperfect.
22. Feels alone and sets self up for it by avoiding relationships.
23. Ultimate act: killing.
24. Seeks self-esteem through titles and badges and seeks the positive from the outside world. Often overlooks the negative aspects of an unknown situation. Grandiose.
25. Focuses on the negative aspects of people and denies their positive values. The perceived weaknesses of others enhances own self-esteem.
26. Left brain dominant. "I'm right, you're wrong."
27. Denies the significance of relationships.

The Lone Rangers see neither their problems nor how they victimize themselves. They don't see their dependency and others don't see it, either. On the surface, Lone Rangers are counterdependent. They deny any dependency. They don't see how perfection is out of balance, or how vulnerable they really are. They don't see that their safety net of apparent self-confidence is just an illusion.

Lone Rangers are the pilots who attempt suicide at retirement or the longshoremen who develop ulcers. They are the workaholic corporate executives, divorced and alone at night, and the law partners who become involved with the secretary. They are the physicians who lose themselves and burn out taking care of patients, and they are the dentists who can't manage their offices.

Lone Rangers' greatest lie to themselves is that everything is okay — they can "handle" it. They don't think they have any problems until they are decked and on the mat. Their counterdependency is the manifestation of their underlying dependency conflicts.

THE HELPLESS VICTIM

All of the miseries of mankind come from one thing, not knowing how to remain alone.
Blaise Pascal
French Philosopher

Each of the inflexible coping patterns, or safety nets, creates problems. Helpless Victims create problems even more obviously than Lone Rangers, because they regularly, in one way or another, refuse to take care of themselves. They want someone else to do it for them. Their prototypical position is one of sacrifice, martyrdom and struggle with all the burdens of this life. They often imply, by action or words, that they are in pain, that they have given much, that they have been hurt and that they are suffering.

Helpless Victims reduce the reality variables in their lives by manipulating others to *care for them* — by finding someone else to handle their reality. They operate on the illusion that if they process their *feelings,* they will ultimately be healed through the catharsis of simply expressing them. They are oriented toward feeling and expression rather than action. They seek to control relationships and avoid external reality, because they believe in their hearts that they aren't capable of taking care of themselves.

Their guru could be Woody Allen as a rag-tattered victim in analysis interminable who plays the blues for everyone to hear. They find solace in having children to raise and correct — people more vulnerable and inadequate than themselves. They want to keep children as children and wish they themselves were children. They complain that their spouses are like children and wait on them compulsively.

Helpless Victims cling dependently to relationships. Refusing to take action, they cry, whine, fuss, complain, gripe and gossip. They are nice. They care. They feel miserable. They set themselves up by repeatedly going into victim situations. Obviously dependent, they hang on to a victim identification. Or, if they fall in love, they become victims .

Often neglectful of their clothing and appearance, Helpless Victims smile wanly through sad eyes. They are relationship-focused and can't stand being alone. They fear rejection and, at the same time, set it up. They need a

relationship to "grow," and thrive on "relationship work."
"Let's work on the relationship" is their battle cry.
Before we go further, let's take a look at the characteristics of the seriously polarized Helpless Victim:

1. Tries to *avoid* external reality.
2. Tries to *control* relationship reality.
3. Disrespects self and excessively respects others.
4. Denies anger and, therefore, accepts fear and sadness.
5. Favorite affect is sadness and favorite attitude is self-pity.
6. Verbal about self and attempts to correct others through guilt — tries to control relationships.
7. Dominated by feelings, usually sadness with hurt. Less logical. Depressed, and manifests dependency in relationships.
8. Wears no mask.
9. With the reality stimulus, the sequence of reaction is feel, act, think. Sometimes it's feel, feel, feel, perhaps act.
10. Imprecise about boundaries. Takes on the problems of others.
11. Words speak louder than actions: "I love you." It's magic phrase. Requires magic words.
12. Needs someone to act as a caretaker for them. Is often a caretaker of children and vulnerable others.
13. Is flexible, easily manipulated, non-critical and feels incompetent.
14. Compulsive caretakee. Feels entitled to be cared for.
15. Tears flow when others don't agree.
16. Unkempt appearance.
17. Blames self: "You don't have a problem, I do." "I'm sorry." "I'm wrong, you're right."
18. Everything is gray. Won't stand up for anything. Values are situationally determined.
19. Feels eternally imperfect.
20. Displays mistakes regularly for all to see.
21. Political groups: any that are organized in such a way that others can overwhelm them — no authority, no chain of command. Other typical groups are

moonies, hippies, and love bombers. Healers by catharsis, through tears and words.
22. Desperately fears being alone and lets everybody know of their fears. Often phobic and avoids reality.
23. Ultimate act is suicide.
24. Emphasizes the positive in people, no matter how limited, and often denies or overlooks the negative.
25. Emphasizes the negative in the outside world due to fear, and denies the positive aspects of the lessons from the outside world.
26. Right brain dominant. Too willing to accept criticism.
27. Denies the significance of the outside world.

Very few of us are as helpless as this list suggests, but if it's clearly described, we can better recognize the specific coping polarity. The theme is the same. Real life with change is frightening, so the variables must be reduced in some way. Helpless Victims need someone to take care of fearsome mastodons and garage mechanics. They stay in relationships, jobs, and organizations, even though they are taken advantage of.

Their lie to themselves is the *same* as the Lone Ranger's — they can take it. They are survivors! Survivors of their own self-victimization. It's all okay. But they have so many problems, they feel no one could ever help them. Their illusion, if they do go into recovery, is passive: that they won't have to take decisive action to change their lives. Just tell another person how they feel, and they'll be better. By somehow simply abiding in a therapeutic situation, a healing event will occur that will transform them. They won't have to take action or actually do anything. They assume that insight alone will bring automatic change and behavior.

Helpless Victims think they are "codependent." Not really understanding what that is, they often read books aimed at defining and healing their suffering. But, in spite of all their serious efforts at recovery and self-understanding, even Helpless Victims often miss the Big Picture.

Upon the most superficial examination, it is easy to see that dependency problems are pervasive. Dependency issues go far beyond the alcoholic or chemically-dependent family. Yes, dependency problems are present in such families — but they are also everywhere else. *You don't have to come from an alcoholic or impaired family to have dependency issues or problems.*

CODEPENDENCY

"Codependency" is a term derived from the chemical dependency literature. Actually, the originally word was "co-alcoholic." If your husband was an alcoholic and you stayed with him while he drank and disrupted the family, you were co-alcoholic with him because, in a sense, you were as dependent on alcohol as he was. With the new term of "chemical dependency," which includes all mind-altering substances, you might then remain with him as a "codependent."

In truth, codependents aren't codependent on anything — they are simply *dependent.* They aren't dependent on the drug or the alcohol but on the *individual,* the *relationship.* They're frightened of the real world and feel helpless to cope with reality and the variables of an ever-changing world. Thus, they become Helpless Victims and find their identity in dependent relationships. It makes no difference whether the partner is drinking or not drinking. Meryl Streep was dependent on Robert Redford in *Out of Africa,* and he was neither an alcoholic nor a drug addict.

It's important to note that this book isn't an argument *against* codependency. It is a clarification of the two polarized dependency patterns (Lone Ranger and Helpless Victim) seen so often in troubled relationships. It is a book that describes codependency as an aspect of a larger order — a Big Picture understanding of life. Consequently, the word "codependency" is avoided in this book, because it's too limited and may create confusion with subsequent recovery plans.

The simple term "dependency" is more operational. The Helpless Victim is obviously dependent on another person.

Lone Rangers are just as dependent as Helpless Victims because they are *counterdependent* and, therefore, also suffering from dependency and vulnerability problems. They simply deny their dependency, while the Helpless Victims exaggerate it. But, because they deny it doesn't mean they aren't dependent. Lone Rangers show their underlying dependency and fear by *avoiding* relationships.

In no way is this book intended to give people additional *word labels* that could themselves be limiting. Its purpose is to give *fundamental metaphoric concepts* upon which to integrate understanding of the balanced and ever-changing larger order. Besides, who wants to be reductionistically labeled as only "codependent," when we're all so much more than that? Unfortunately, the term "codependency" has come to represent all the defensive positions and thus makes the recovery process confusing.

CONNECTION

The Lone Ranger and Helpless Victim — two protective, illusion-fostering patterns of life — are very similar. Each seems different on the surface, but their foundations are the same. The two patterns are *connected* in that they are based on the same vulnerability, dependency, and fear of change. We may handle it differently, but we are all somewhat frightened. We don't see our own lack of balance or our vain attempts to hide from the lessons that are there for us to learn. Indeed, some pass through life without ever learning the lessons. Others may catch a glimpse of the larger order in their later years or perhaps on their death bed. The fact is that the two polarities — the Longer Ranger and Helpless Victim — are safety net illusions that simply do not work over time.

We use these relationship attachment patterns against the reality of relationship evolution and change. One of these two polarized positions may reveal the foundation of your own fear, need for safety, and avoidance. They are primitive sub-specializations that no longer work in the contemporary family of humanity. If you choose to stay with these defenses, you will find yourself alone and in pain — because *both are victim positions.* Both result in rejection because *no one wants to be with a victim.* Although victims may appear responsible for others, they are irresponsible with themselves. Lone Rangers become especially angry with other victims who remind them of their own underlying vulnerability and victimhood. Lone Ranger perfectionists are boring and obnoxious, while Helpless Victims can become obviously parasitic. Both polarities are demanding and, thereby, encourage rejection.

As caretakers, we seek the vulnerability in others to heal ourselves. At the same time, we victimize ourselves through the unbalanced care of others. As caretakees, we seek the invulnerability in someone else to heal our own vulnerability, but we victimize ourselves and make ourselves even more vulnerable in the process.

With this introduction to the larger picture, you should begin to see portions of the pathway to your own balance, your own inner healing. None of us uses Lone Ranger or Helpless Victim patterns 100 percent of the time. But, if we do use such defensive patterns, we will find ourselves, ultimately, in pain. Even if we use these defenses only five, 10, or 15 percent of the time, that small percentage can become our undoing. Because a ten-percent problem can quickly developed into a 100-percent tragedy.

If you have a car with one spark plug burned out, how far will it go? If you're dressed to go out and realize you have no shoes, will you go? Can you see how a small 10-percent problem can ruin an entire activity?

If we can begin to understand the intimacy, the profound *connections* that exist between these two polarities, we can enhance the healing process. There are, of course, Lone Ranger women and Helpless Victim men. There are no sexual sub-groups, no "women's or men's issues" — only our personal drives to avoid and control different aspects of the real world.

Paradoxically, control is a form of avoidance and avoidance is a form of control. If we work too hard to *control* relationships, we end up *avoiding* the consequences of the relationship reality. And the act of *avoiding* relationships gives us a measure of security and *control.*

We all find ourselves, from time to time, stuck in the illusion of safety. We're all guilty of emphasizing differences and making comparisons in an effort to make things logical — black and white. Categorizing is a form of escape and of relapse. Practicing techniques of avoidance and control temporarily helps us cope with the outside world and the intimacy of relationships while we search for ways to understand and cope with what we cannot change. We all must ultimately deal directly with the natural reality of our relationships. Each of us has the same opportunity to use our relationship realities to seek balance in our lives — something we all want to find.

We are all seeking balance and peace. When you get right down to it, we humans are all the same.

5

Bedroom To Boardroom Combinations:

Defensive Patterns In
Different Relationships

*When I die and come before the throne of God he
will ask not why I was not like Abraham, why I was
not like Issac or Moses — he will ask why was I not
more like Martin Buber.*

*Martin Buber, 20th Century
Jewish Philosopher*

IN DIFFERENT REALITY CIRCUMSTANCES, we often find
ourselves in the same perplexing predicament as Martin
Buber. We don't behave in a manner representative of our
personal values.

Upon even superficial self-evaluation, most people can
clearly identify with either the Lone Ranger or Helpless
Victim defensive patterns. Others may see themselves as
having characteristics of both, depending upon the situation. The fact is that if you're out of balance, you're going
to defensively swing one way or another, and it may not always be the same way.

Balance is the healthy, aware, middle ground. It represents an ongoing, appropriate adjustment to changing con-

temporary reality: No further expectations ... no entitlement ... therefore no problems. Just as in the earlier story
in which different people reacted differently to the same
snake, so can the same person react differently to each reality situation depending upon their perceptions and their
life experience.

We all waiver between balance and imbalance. While
most of our lives are balanced, we are never *entirely* balanced. Each new reality situation has the potential to
throw us off if we exhibit excessive attachment (control) or
excessive retreat (avoidance). And if we are out of balance
even 10 percent, it throws off the 90 percent that is
healthy and reasonable.

The biggest difficulty we face as individuals, or as a society, is how we regularly permit ourselves to remain out of
balance. It's how quickly we panic when we feel we're out
of control and can no longer avoid reality. It's how we
throw ourselves out of balance in all of our relationships
from bedroom to boardroom.

Often, people come into my office and tell me about the
areas of their lives in which they do well. That's like taking a car with a dented fender to the body repair shop and
showing the repairman how well the radio works. What's
the point? And just as rust eats away at a dented fender,
your problems slowly begin to wear on you. They drain
your self-esteem. Before you know it, a small 10-percent
problem requires a major 100-percent solution. The larger
problem could have been avoided with a little
maintenance.

Balance activity is maintenance. It transcends situations and is above fear. It accepts natural reality. Balance
is objectively detached and yet is aware of and connected
to the motion of change. Feelings occur, but they are handled from a perspective of detachment and responsibility.

INTIMACY

Intimacy, in its various forms, can easily kick us out of
balance. We want intimacy, and yet we fear it. We pursue

it, and yet we run from it. We are hurt by changes in levels and types of intimacy.

We are all capable of using either the Lone Ranger or Helpless Victim defensive patterns in any of our personal relationships as a means of coping with real or imagined changes in intimacy. Each relationship, personal or group, is experienced differently in terms of intimacy, commitment and change. We can either be over-involved or under-involved. No matter where you are in life, at work or at home, different types and degrees of intimacy have the potential to create conflicts.

Work relationships may, at times, be more *verbally* intimate than marital relationships. Conversely, personal relationships may sometimes be predominantly *physically* intimate. People may spend a great deal of time together without being verbal or physically intimate. Sadly, even some couples who are sexually intimate fail to be verbally intimate. It's an odd comment on our relationships that people can make "love" without ever discussing their paycheck, their mortgage, or their HIV (an AIDS test) results. Physical intimacy, often synonymous with love, is only one aspect of a relationship.

There are three different types of intimacy: Verbal, physical and bonding.

Verbal intimacy can include all types of personal information exchanges that range from telling simple things about yourself, such as what part of the country you're from, to telling your most shameful secrets. Interestingly, what people are ashamed of varies remarkably. I talked with one former patient for two years before she told me the burning secret that her uncle's first wife had been a prostitute. Now, this secret was not relevant on the surface, but it clearly was important to her. Most secrets are shame-based. The thinking goes "I, or someone in my family, did something wrong, and if I tell you, you will think I'm defective." Maintaining secrets about life events is much like painting over a rusted dent. The secret may cover the pain. But the pain cannot be repaired unless some honest connections occur through verbal intimacy.

Honest talk and an objective review lead to a transcendent outcome.

Acquiring the perspective of the larger order will assist you in discussing secrets. Secrets yield valuable lessons — if you perceive the lesson process.

Physical intimacy ranges from sharing the same home or work area with someone to engaging in sexual acts. A hug or a touch on the shoulder is physically more intimate than not touching. In studying the sexual addictions, it's interesting to see how the level of addiction depends upon the level of intimacy. The levels range from compulsive, agreed-upon intimacy with others, to compulsive intimacy that is not at all agreed upon, and that is, in fact, criminal intrusion. It's clear that respectful contact builds trust. Disrespectful physical contact builds resentment.

Bonding is the healthy, balanced intimacy that occurs over time. It is based on commitment, respect and appreciation for the other person's developmental struggles. It's an appreciation of your partner's boundaries. It creates a partnership of mutual growth, individual responsibility and little victimhood.

Unbalanced bonding creates relationship victims. Victims are controlling and demanding even when they are silent. Bonding can become a problem if it results in an exclusive, fixed and limited relationship. In such a situation, couples may judge others negatively and eliminate other activities in relationships. Such "relationship evolution" without personal evolution in the outside world is unbalanced and will ultimately prove to be characterized by underlying fear and dependency. The couple, the family and the corporation will suffer from that kind of insular attitude. The purpose of such exclusive bonding is for safety; it is not for enhanced development.

In the larger order, each of us is responsible for our own self-development in the context of many different relationships. Balanced levels of intimacy in different types of relationships can serve as a barometer for relationship evolution. As relationships evolve, people should become *more* respectful of the other person's boundaries, not *less* respectful. Some incorrectly assume that "love" means a kind of accepting permission and an opportunity to be less respectful as the relationship evolves.

Each individual or group relationship in our lives can be characterized by the level or degree of intimacy in it. Unbalanced patterns of intimacy can be characterized by either inappropriate emotional isolation or dependent vulnerability. The defensive pendulum of life can swing either way. Non-awareness of, or inattention to, this simple fact will create victim situations in *any* personal relationship.

Through these self-created victim roles we can learn relationship balance. If we're too dependent upon intimacy or too counterdependent (isolating ourselves and fearing intimacy), we can use those patterns for our lesson process.

A young couple once came to see me because they were unsure whether or not to get married. They loved each other but had one major difference between them. She was a woman who loved to talk, share feelings and *then* enjoy physical intimacy. She looked forward to bonding over time. He, on the other hand, wanted to get physical first and talk later. As I listened to them, it was easy to see what their problem was. They were out of sync.

I told them about the three levels of intimacy, and numbered them 1) physical, 2) verbal and 3) bonding. I explained to the woman that she was a 2-1-3 sequence person and that his sequence was 1-2-3.

"No Doc," he said, "you've got it wrong. I'm actually a 1-1-1 person." That's a true story, by the way. At any rate, the couple did get married. Years later, they came back with the same problem. They were each still fighting for their own timing sequence. Their unmet personal needs continued to prohibit bonding, and they had difficulty with trust because they fought over the sequence in the types of intimacy. Their conflict was over *inconsistent* intimacy and *inconsistent* boundaries, with poorly negotiated boundary management. There was little agenda compromise.

With these observations, one can begin to understand why the boss runs off with the secretary. He talks to her all day, so she knows all his problems. They share common goals. She knows more about the business than his wife. He feels closer to her than to his wife. They are *verbally intimate*. They connect on issues, are respectful of each other's agendas, and seek to understand each other's communications. They develop skills of compromise. They have delineated, agreed upon areas of control over one another. Their boundaries are relatively *consistent* because they have agreed upon levels of intimacy. But, there may be little compromise in the agenda at home.

Levels of *physical intimacy* can vary with a couple. I once knew a young college student who was madly in love. He was sexually involved with his girlfriend, but only to the point of heavy petting. As will happen, on one occasion the petting began to advance to a higher level of intimacy. "I'll never see you again," she said. He took it as an admonition: "I'll leave you if you go further." Later, he realized that wasn't what she meant at all. She, too, feared rejection and was asking for reassurance that their intimacy wouldn't lead to his abandonment of her. She had verbalized the rejection they both feared. As the physical intimacy progressed, the possibility of rejection presented a new relationship reality for both of them. *Both* feared the new level of intimacy. Interestingly, she wanted verbal reassurance and verbal commitment as physical intimacy progressed.

I've seen many couples become quite angry and controlling soon after marriage. The profound verbal vows and the increased physical intimacy encourage the couple to feel more committed, more responsible. But, this new state of intimacy and commitment is too frightening, and so the defenses go up. Arguments occur where there had previously been patience, compromise and understanding.

Healthy verbal and physical intimacy respects self and others. It adjusts to changes. Unhealthy intimacy is repetitively frozen, consumptive, or defensive.

BALANCE: INTIMACY AND BEING ALONE

Intuitively, we all know we're alone. We're born alone and we die alone. Many struggle most of their lives to overcome the feeling of being alone. Ultimately, our most important choices are made alone, and it is in such choices that we can find valuable developmental lesson opportunities. It is true that "shared" choices do integrate more information and more experience. But, in the end, your decisions are your own. Unbalanced choices, made through unbalanced submission to others, may be a way to avoid full responsibility and learning.

In an effort to overcome the discomfort of being alone, we either seek connections with each other or seek to be alone to deny our fears of isolation. At times, we seek intimacy to avoid responsibility. We seek the person or the group to make the decision for us. Relationship connections can be balanced, offering a chance for further communication and understanding, or they can be unbalanced, locked into false connections and frozen relationship attachments and expectations. These frozen attachments replace true understanding.

For example, two people talking negatively and judgmentally about another share false intimacy and a false connection: gossip. Such patter is both reassuring and destructive. In gossip, there is no resolution, no decision and no action; there is only momentary satisfaction and safety. Because it offers reassurance, gossip can become addictive.

On the other hand, two people discussing an event or another person with an aim at understanding themselves or others through objective analysis are alive — they are developmentally connected. That kind of transcendent process can lead to correct action. They learn to objectify their perceptions and stabilize their reactions.

The way we talk to each other can reveal a great deal about our patterns. Helpless Victims try to connect by *complaining*. If they find another victim to agree, their conversation becomes gossip. Or, they may find another victim with whom to compare suffering.

"You think you had it bad — let me tell you how bad it is for me!" This is victim competition, a victim war. "My suffering is worse than yours," etc., etc. This interaction does not encourage understanding. Such a comparison process is dualistic and seeks labels. Comparisons are both categorical and reductionistic. Recovery is self-reflective and objective, not negatively discriminating.

Lone Rangers are more likely to connect intellectually. They might use concepts or abstractions, but nothing on a personal level. They are connected cognitively, not by affect or by awareness of vulnerability. They don't want you to know who they are for fear of sounding like a victim. They play their cards close to the vest, always appearing confident and perfect. They don't understand personal problems — they've never had one. They can't understand you, because they can't understand themselves.

If Lone Rangers or Helpless Victims seek out people with these same defensive operations, they keep themselves separated and disconnected from others through evolved defensive wordplay. True self-understanding in such relationships rarely takes place — they feed into each other. Instead, feelings of anger, impatience, isolation or depression are common. Through repetitive patterns, they remain alone and become more desperate over time. They remain in their own self-created quagmire — their own gossip subgroup — locked in the trap of comparing themselves to others.

Intimacy or connections, at any level, cannot replace deeper understanding. To be physically close is reassuring and to be verbally open can be a relief. But, true understanding brings the opportunity for personal evolution through balanced action — through directly facing the present relationship reality.

Back when I was in medical school, a psychiatrist confided to our class that he and his wife regularly achieved mutual orgasm. Nevertheless, they were getting a divorce. He said they shared "intimacy" and satisfaction but had no personal connection or understanding. He, himself, demonstrated little self-awareness and seemed detached and inappropriate in his comments. After he told the class these intimate details, we wondered if he had been connected at all. He had little respect for his appropriate marital boundaries. His problem with his wife reflected his problem with himself.

NEEDS

So many relationship disappointments are based on the concept of "needs." Many people expect their "needs" to be met in a relationship. Pain results when that doesn't happen. Let's face this point realistically at the outset — our needs are *not* always met.

That brings to mind a song sung by Mick Jagger and the Rolling Stones which tells us we can't always get what we want, but if we try real hard, we might just *sometimes* get what we need.

Note the word "sometimes." We all have "needs," but we must be careful when they become "demands." Some say, "Forget about what you *want,* and just go for what you *need.*" But this remark encourages the illusion that a "need" is justifiable because it is more powerful than a "want," and, therefore, it must be met. I know many drug addicts who *need* their drug, just as some people *need* that love from someone else. The *need* becomes so intense that the person becomes indiscriminate in seeking to satisfy it.

A friend told me a story about my namesake Charlie (The Bird) Parker, the great jazz saxophonist who died of a heroin overdose. After a performance one night, Charlie felt the "need." He turned to my friend and said desperately, "Man have you got *anything?*"

If we look for *needs* to be satisfied, we can get demanding and indiscriminate just like poor Charlie. But, if we search for balance, we will find ourselves less driven and more able to give and receive. If we go looking for satisfaction and don't receive it, what will we do? Can we handle not receiving, or will we crank it up and become demanding?

If we truly *want* something in our life, we should work for it and earn it for ourselves. It will come if we just let go of the *demanding* — if we just let go of the *need.*

Many years ago, when I was a medical intern in Grand Rapids, Michigan, I developed a theory called the *"Theory of Circumvential Direction."* During that difficult year, I lost my self chasing painful relationship expectations which regularly evaded my grasp. Working frequent 36-

hour shifts, I was so burned out, I was burned in. Late one night, in the midst of a spring thunderstorm, I went outside the emergency room for a breath of air. It was there that the theory came to me in a grand illumination:

> If we believe there is a treasure in the woods and run madly through those woods looking for it, we will surely die of exposure and exhaustion before we find it. If, however, each of us takes the time to walk slowly through the woods and enjoy the trees, the mushrooms and the natural events — if we connect with the natural order — we will ultimately walk into a clearing and find the treasure we seek. One must have a visualization of the goals, but being grabby and demanding is self-defeating.

It wasn't until much later that I learned my theory wasn't original. The concept was more than 2,000 years old. The Zen Masters long ago taught that successful travel in this trip of life can be accomplished through *acceptance* and not through attachments. Therefore, I suggest we drop all the "wants" and "needs" discussion and settle for the less demanding term "preferences." In recovery meetings, we must come to see the dependency of "needs" and "wants."

GROUP SUBTYPES

In discussing relationship realities, we can simplify the discussion by separating them into two subtypes: individual relationships and group relationships. Individual relationships tend to be more intimate with fewer obvious variables (only the variables one person presents), while groups are often less intimate with many more variables (the reality variables of many). That, of course, is why public speaking and leadership are difficult. The myriad of relationship variables in groups is increased, the risk of rejection is greater. Rejection from an individual, on the other hand, may at times be more painful to bear, because that person may have greater significance than the group.

The degree to which people are balanced in either group or personal relationships depends on a variety of issues such as life experience, previous hurts and childhood programming. As we swing out of balance in either type of relationship, we show our insecurities by using either the Lone Ranger or Helpless Victim coping system. Which one we use may depend on the situation. For example, a person may be a Lone Ranger (LR) caretaker at work — strong, a bit aloof and controlling. But, that same person may go home and play the Helpless Victim (HV) role in the personal relationships there.

In Chapter 4, we described the *Lone Ranger and Helpless Victim* defensive activities in personal relationships. Now, let's take a look at these same defensive patterns as they are expressed in work/groups. As we start, remember that work and the outside world are a *mixture* of group experiences and individual experiences. If a person becomes emotionally closer and more verbally or physically intimate with specific colleagues, some of the Chapter 4 patterns will present themselves. In other words, different types of relationship vulnerabilities and perceived realities result in different types of defenses.

THE WORK/GROUP LONE RANGER

Most people find groups are more intimidating than individuals. In a work setting, Lone Rangers follow some of the same patterns as they do in personal relationships. To cope with their fear of the group, they try to reduce the number of variables by exhibiting the following types of behaviors:

1. Prefers a strong vertical work organization. ("I'm the boss.")
2. Emphasizes charisma and appearance.
3. Uses posturing, posing and non-verbal hand signals.
4. Uses strong caretaker verbalizations: "I will take care of you, if you are vulnerable or fall."
5. Intimidated by strong internal opposition. Distrustful.

6. Never tells anyone what he does (everyone is dispensable but him). Self-centered.
7. Frequently lies, and close associates know it.
8. Manipulates people by dangling carrots, only to withdraw them later.
9. Avoids being put on the line. If it happens, uses power dressing and an entourage for impression management.
10. Rigid, grandiose and entitled. Takes credit for everything: "The organization is me."
11. Disrespectful to others with anger and shouting, but permits no disrespect toward self.
12. Looks for perks — sets others up as personal caretakers.
13. Plays favorites, but is fickle with employees.
14. Is a workaholic, and will likely have other dependencies.
15. May have office affairs, using power and position to take advantage of students, trainees, etc. Has problems with sexual conduct, sexual boundaries.
16. Makes intuitive and capricious decisions — nothing goes to committee. Own mistakes are "interesting." Others' mistakes are "serious."
17. Won't take on a mentor role because it risks intimacy. Can't correct others in a balanced way or raise a successor. At times, a destructive humorist. If you get close, you'll be banished for your imperfection.
18. Often avoids public presentations, because a mistake might crack the illusion of perfection. Denies fear.
19. Marriage is tertiary to work and power.

THE WORK/GROUP HELPLESS VICTIM

At work, Helpless Victims are more hidden and subtle, but still identifiable if you look for them. They too, are fearful of the group and try to decrease the variables by having someone else take the responsibility. The following are typical characteristics:

1. A go-fer — plays behind the scenes as a helper.
2. Works excessively but refuses credit.
3. Assumes any problems are due to own lack of insight.
4. Constantly asks, "How am I doing?"
5. Shy and fearful of group discussion.
6. Exhibits poor grooming and often has a weight problem.
7. Wants to be in control, but tries to manage through "niceness and helpfulness."
8. Assumes people will like them because they smile and say hello.
9. An inveterate gossip. Will talk about anything or anybody (judgmental of others).
10. Cries when confronted about issues of indecisiveness.
11. Everyone's mentor and protector — points out the difficulty of own job.
12. Feels misunderstood and hurt by those who are administratively senior.
13. Feels inferior. Displays poor eye contact, little confidence and won't negotiate a raise.
14. Can't make a decision. Always confused. Everything must go to a committee. Talks too much.
15. After committee makes a recommendation, still can't decide.
16. Poor at setting personal boundaries, agendas or scheduling of own time. Can't prioritize.
17. Never appears to be irritated or insulted. Always smiles and hides true feelings — hides any negativity. Laughs regularly at self in public.
18. Avoids public presentations to avoid answering questions.
19. Job role is only source of personal identity.

Remember this: no one likes a victim. Victims, whether Lone Rangers or Helpless Victims, behave irresponsibly with others and with themselves. Their irresponsibility is a burden for the group. A Lone Ranger hot dog is controlling, demanding, out of bounds and manipulative — destined to irritate others and go down in victim flames. The

Helpless Victim, also struggling for control, alienates others by whining and complaining. No one wants to be around either a hot dog or a whiner. The struggle for control bodes an unhappy ending. Such struggles, either active or passive, encourage a victim outcome.

To be in balance, the Lone Ranger must detach from the safety of the ivory tower and *connect to committed relationships*. The Helpless Victim must emotionally detach from relationship dependencies and *connect with the outside world*. Balance activity is different for each.

THE COMBINATIONS

If we place the work/outside group defenses on the top and our personal defensive patterns on the bottom, we find four possible combinations of the two defensive patterns as in the diagram below:

Group relationship **LONE RANGER**	$\left(\begin{array}{c} LR \\ LR \end{array}\right)$	
Personal relationship **LONE RANGER**		
(Lost child)		

Group relationship **LONE RANGER**	$\left(\begin{array}{c} LR \\ HV \end{array}\right)$	
Personal relationship **HELPLESS VICTIM**		
(Hero)		

Group relationship **HELPLESS VICTIM**	$\left(\begin{array}{c} HV \\ LR \end{array}\right)$	
Personal relationship **LONE RANGER**		
(Mascot)		

Group relationship **HELPLESS VICTIM**	$\left(\begin{array}{c} HV \\ HV \end{array}\right)$	
Personal relationship **HELPLESS VICTIM**		
(Scapegoat)		

It is noteworthy that the HV/HV and the LR/LR are the least balanced, most polarized individuals. The other two subtypes are trying to balance themselves, as they are less locked into any one position. Think about your own patterns of behavior at work and at home. Can you determine your combination? Of course, keep in mind that none of these patterns is fixed. People characteristically find themselves changing according to circumstance. A Lone Ranger/Lone Ranger may at other times be a Lone Ranger/Helpless Victim, depending on the variable of personal relationship differences.

After working with these four combinations for a couple of years, it occurred to me that they were not unlike the dependency patterns discussed elsewhere in the recovery literature for alcoholic families. In dysfunctional families, there are four basic subtype patterns in the children: the hero, the mascot, the lost child and the scapegoat. These dependency patterns are fairly obvious and are not only found in children of alcoholics, but in any dysfunctional family. "Dysfunctional," I should say here, is synonymous with "unbalanced." *All* families are, to some degree, dysfunctional in their approach to real change. The word "dysfunctional" is too negative, categorical and reductionistic. It sets up defensive patterns. Rather than use "dysfunctional" or "impaired," we can address any degree of dysfunction or impairment by looking at aspects of the family that are out of balance.

The Lone Ranger/Helpless Victim pattern is that of the family *hero,* controlled and achievement-oriented on the outside, jelly on the inside. These people, strong and competent at work, are insecure at home or in close, personal relationships. They are rescuers, caretakers, protectors — but they can't take care of themselves. The needs of others are so predominant in their personal lives that they have little ability to find themselves or to make their own choices. They struggle to look good. They can't set limits on people with whom they are intimate. If heroes have an eating disorder, it's likely to be bulimia. If they use chemicals, they choose cocaine or alcohol. As an example of the hero, think of world leaders who are caretakers but who can't set limits on their own team.

The Helpless Victim/Lone Ranger pattern represents the family *mascot,* always happy and joking on the outside. They try to make everything funny. Nothing appears serious to them, and they compulsively laugh throughout their lives, poking fun at themselves and others. But inside they are alone and desperate in their efforts to not be rejected. Some comedians will come right out and say it: "Just love me. Don't reject me." Such individuals are disconnected and alone on a personal level, searching for a supportive connection with a group of people. They may use amphetamines, cocaine or alcohol. As examples, think of the comedians who die alone.

The Lone Ranger/Lone Ranger is the *lost child.* These people are alone, distant, angry, sullen and depressed. If they have an eating disorder, it will be anorexia. They have been hurt and can't bounce back — they can't risk connection. Usually, this type is negative, judgmental, sarcastic and supercilious. They are the drifters of this world, and they can't speak, act or feel. They appear sullen, introspective and silent. They may become so reclusive that they begin to look like victims. Their addictions are often alcohol or heroin. Think of the many actors and musicians who kill themselves with sex, drugs and alcohol.

Last, but not least, are the *scapegoats* — Helpless Victims/Helpless Victims. They ask for trouble, and they don't care how they present themselves to others. As adolescents, they look like "grits" or "heads." Always too loud, they complain too much and cry in their beer. They seek out victim situations, create them when necessary, and then complain even more. They always expect to gain respect without effort. They disdain structure and authority. Such victims as these ultimately become demanding and imperious — just like Lone Rangers. Their drugs of choice are pot, hallucinogens, alcohol ... anything. As an example, think of the disheveled "rebels" who scream their despair.

Notice that these subgroups contain puzzling aspects of both Lone Ranger and Helpless Victim defensive polarities, and that the specific combination depends on the particular group or personal relationship realities. Again, it's important to emphasize that these subgroup combinations, just as the original Lone Ranger and Helpless Victim, are not absolute, 100-percent categories. These are guidelines only for self-reflection, not for the analysis of others.

It is helpful, in our effort to understand these behaviors, to abandon Aristotelian, black-and-white thinking and recognize these constructs as Einsteinian constellations. They are aggregates, *behavioral fields of activity,* rather than fixed entities. These are not precisely measurable forms. And by thinking of them as tonal patterns or trends in behavior occurring over time, we can begin to see the problems in our polarized, unbalanced responses to relationship reality.

Furthermore, using a "field" conceptualization allows us to include aspects of functioning in which the person is balanced and doing well. That way, we can avoid categorical, negative judgments and apparent name calling such as "You're (just a) codependent." "You're from a (completely) dysfunctional family." "You're (only) an alcoholic." "You're (just) a Lone Ranger."

It's important for you to understand that the terms "Lone Ranger and Helpless Victim" are designed as metaphors or descriptive constellations that can themselves be discarded once the fundamental, operational defensive series is understood. They are not designed to create new, reductionistic catch phrases that limit and codify people, but rather as metaphoric maps that will take us beyond our limited, previous field of vision. Furthermore, this breakdown of combinations should not be discussed with your lover or work associates. *It's for you to use for yourself.* You will meet with resistance and create a victim role for yourself if you attempt to use these ideas in an effort to correct others. It will not help for you to tell someone else what they should do. They may reject your suggestions because they perceive them as controlling or, conversely, they may try hard *for you,* rather than for themselves, and *blame* you when you don't appreciate their efforts. Your loved ones have to first see and feel their *own* pain, before they can make the effort to seek balance. It's not your place to tell them about their pain. If they ask, perhaps you can give them this book. But don't use these new concepts to get caught in the caretaker dependency trap.

THE VARIABLES

Each of these four patterns differ according to the way we perceive each relationship situation. We often perceive groups and individuals as either supportive or intimidating. Therefore, a person may be predominantly a LR in some group self-management, but may become an HV with other specific groups. In a similar way, a person may be predominantly a LR in almost all personal relationships, but an HV in selected, more intimate personal relationships. The patterns change according to the issues of fear and low self-esteem present in each situation.

One woman, whom I have seen professionally, is a marked LR in all personal and group relationships, save one. She is a definite LR/LR — negativistic, angry, controlling and judgmental. But with her father, she is apologetic, never angry and always seeking to please. She tries to *control* all relationships in her life — but tries to *avoid* tensions with her father. In doing so, she has created a victim role for herself in each situation.

RELATIONSHIP CATCH-22: YOU CAN'T WIN

Every dependency-oriented relationship, whether it's predominantly LR or HV, presents a catch-22 situation for the partner or group involved, because of the dependent person's obvious desire to control. Some people believe opposites attract. Others say we're attracted to those similar to ourselves. But, the truth is that we select partners who present possible resolutions of our own destructive patterns. *We select them to help us evolve, and we resent them when they try to change us.* We select relationship realities that fit our defensive patterns and our level of self-esteem evolution. Relationships become a catch-22 when you discover that, in terms of your partner or your group, you're damned either way. You're trapped. You can't please them. If you're involved and concerned, you're "too weak." If you make suggestions, you're "too controlling." *You* are perceived as causing *their* problems. *They* would feel better, if only *you* could correct *your* foolish ways.

You can come to see your *self* through your victim patterns in your relationships. If a Lone Ranger wants to develop a personal, intimate relationship, he will have expectations of his partner that aren't obvious. Those often unconscious expectations might lead the Lone Ranger to feel there is either too much or too little intimacy in the relationship. He will judge her as he does himself. He doesn't make his own internal adjustment to the partner and the relationship. Instead, he manipulates her as he does the external world — for his own comfort. He judges his partner's "progress" according to the degree of his own comfort. Meanwhile, the partner keeps trying to jump through hoops to please him, but, of course, she isn't perfect.

Until the Lone Ranger understands that *he's* the uncomfortable one, he'll keep trying to change her in order to make himself comfortable. But it doesn't work that way. The change has to come from within himself — not from his partner — and she must recognize the catch-22 as partly her responsibility.

People, in either the bedroom or boardroom, can exert unhealthy catch-22 control over their associates. Even governments can do it to their people. It happened in China. The Chinese government said, in essence, "It's okay to lighten up. Forget all that repressive cultural revolution stuff — be creative." So women started wearing flowered skirts and the society began to change. The catch-22 for the Chinese people was that they went too far and threatened the security of the leadership. Those in power became uncomfortable and frightened for their safety and job security. They had been pushed out of their own narrow comfort zone. So they turned on the citizenry and hundreds died in the ensuing confrontations. Noteworthy in the pre-massacre period of time was the lack of reasonable, *balanced* win-win communication and negotiation. The national leadership fearfully polarized in a defensive LR position with its own people.

Corporate life works much the same way. There are some, unfortunately, with administrative responsibility to whom the act of firing people is a pleasure — a coup. It's a power trip for them. They give a person a job only to change it two, three or more times. If the employee doesn't adapt well enough or quickly enough — Bam! Out the door. It's a catch-22. The "managers" think they're perfect and that those below them are not. Of course, they don't discuss options with the employee. They simply see problems and clean house. They don't prune or trim their garden as time goes by; they uproot and replant the whole thing. No maintenance. Dispensable people. It's a Styrofoam-cup personnel plan.

No maintenance, no balance, no continuity and no balanced field of behavioral synergy. These are the kinds of control problems one sees in strong vertical organizations where one person stands at the helm and capriciously makes decisions. The entire company group is based only on the chief's comfort zone.

Edward deBono, an international expert on creativity, has observed differing practices and management philosophies as he has consulted with the leadership of international corporations in Japan and the United States. He finds that leaders in the two countries think differently. Japanese management will look at something that isn't going well and say, "That's good, now lets do something different." The Americans are more inclined to say, "Let's can the whole mess and start over." We throw out the cabinet and the cabinet maker. This latter view is an example of reductionistic, primitive, non-creative thinking. It fails to deal with the positive and negative simultaneously, in a balanced way, or to accept the field of behavior. We reductionistically think that we can only handle one thing at a time.

In a similar way, some people in chemical dependency treatment programs believe that they must have only one focus — the chemicals. The problem is that protracted focus on only one aspect of recovery fails to integrate the whole psychological dependency network of denial and defensiveness into the recovery process. More traditional counselors may overlook the positive energy and healing that could take place by seeing the whole field — not just the relationships in which a person is dependently fixated — but relationships in which that same person handles things well. *Every single developmental situation in individual, corporate or national life intrinsically has the potential for both progress and problems. There are no categorical solutions. Each action or inaction has a consequence.*

The Berlin Wall is down and the Soviet Union is now making some effort to be more communicative with its people and with the world. Previously, mistakes were covered up. The Communist block, once awash with lies and deceptions, is finally allowing us to see some of its accidents and problems. News about Chernobyl may have been embarrassing, but it was the only way out of a rusted-shut political system. The Soviets are becoming part of the human community. They now are beginning to take ownership of their own mistakes. They cannot evolve as a nation without that kind of self-examination.

A political system is a work group of sorts. It undergoes internal changes when the political/management system lies about controls and misrepresents itself to the people. When leaders act as caretakers for associates who break the rules, there is a price to pay. Actually, an attempt to portray the leadership group as being perfect, is itself an act of victimhood. Our Vietnam experience was a caretaking, paternalistic, Lone Ranger debacle in which our "perfect" system was imposed on an "imperfect" system.

Personally, I thank God for the refreshing George Bush — "warts and all." He can admit that he isn't perfect. He can dress casually and stand in the surf fishing. He's human. He's real. He seeks balance.

There are, of course, many countries in this world that are defensively stuck in "perfect" positions. These nations have charismatic leaders who rule with coercion and propaganda. Their decisions are swift and self-serving. They strive to isolate their people from the larger world order by convincing them that they are special, different or entitled.

In contrast, some of our "leaders" in business operate as victims. Frozen in indecision, they don't stay leaders long. Because they are out of balance, they repetitively seek advice before sticking their toes in the water. Their decisions are made by group or committee. These are the folks who joke about leadership, titles, protocol, structure and order. A group with this kind of leadership can be confused and slow, because it's too horizontal in its organization. It is unbalanced and argues against the natural order of growth and organizational responsibility.

Leaders who lead by excessive control or by avoidance ultimately will lose their power. In the natural order, leaders and their groups share a negotiated vision of the future.

VULNERABILITY FOOTBALL: RAPID ROLE REVERSALS

In relationships at any level, we often see the phenomena of *vulnerability football*. To deny our own vulnerability, we must believe that someone else has the problem or has caused the problem. For example, one partner, who feels he is in the victim (HV) role, may reflect on his condition and begin to practice more appropriately assertive and detached action. As that person becomes stronger, he will often flip over into an exceedingly strong and tyrannical LR role with his partner. Interestingly, his partner reacts by becoming an HV who begs to keep the relationship going and regrets all her previous wrongdoings.

In another situation, a strong LR may become reflective and begin to deal with his underlying pain, only to flip over into a victim orientation. In response, the partner who had previously been a victim will do a turn-about and begin dispensing advice, giving suggestions and treating the original LR as a child.

As dialogues of this kind heat up between a couple, what often occurs is the ultimate dependency argument.

Vulnerability, pain and the "blame" get passed quickly back and forth between the two individuals: "You hurt me." "Yes, but you hurt me more."

Translated this means, "You're the cause of my pain." "Yes, but you caused my pain first and more intensely." At its worst, this argument degenerates into name calling: "You're a jerk." "Oh yeah, well you're a bigger jerk."

These angry remarks really say, "You are disrespectful and inconsiderate. I can't handle the pain of you treating me that way." The retort, of course, is exactly the same. But such blame is the basis of irresponsible behavior. It's victim war again. Remember: *you're responsible for your own feelings.*

Any angry argument indicates that you've lost your calm. If you're arguing without self-management, you are likely caught up in a dependency. Because you're hurt, you feel entitled to change the other person through guilt, so you're telling him that he caused your pain. But the truth is that *you* caused your pain. *Your* expectations, *your* desires and *your* wish to avoid change caused your pain. "You hurt me" is a statement of blame. People who make such statements are not assuming responsibility for their own lives. They are attempting to use provoking manipulation to change the other person. But we've already agreed that the other person *isn't going to change unless he desires change for himself.* So, it's pointless to try.

> *An angry argument is a loss of the larger perspective. Those who are good at knighthood are not militaristic, those who are good at battle do not become angry, those who are good at prevailing over opponents do not get involved.*
> Lao Tzu, Chinese Philosopher

Detachment will encourage a win-win perspective. Attachment to the outcome, to the wish for the other to change, will bring disappointment. The real issue is the process — the relationship synergy — not the outcome.

It is a fact of reality that pure disrespect does exist. In my role as a hospital consultant, I often see unhealthy polarizations that promote stasis and lack of creativity in

various organizations. Those polarizations can exist anywhere within the organization. They occur when, for example, a hospital patient community separates itself into
non-healing categorical groups: blacks/whites, profession-
als/non-professionals, alcoholics/addicts, chemical depen-
dents/codependents, males/females. At the core of this
problem is always a powerful, unbalanced and entitled
Lone Ranger shouting demands, struggling for control and
pointing out various offenses. He refuses to accept his responsibilities and is in denial. The entire patient population will spin into frightened separate subgroups because
of the fear that such a person encourages. Organizations
and nations often show the same characteristics.

Some people are racially prejudiced. Others have religious prejudices and some are pure xenophobics. Such
people are not living in balance. They are struggling for
safety through avoidance. They fear connecting dialogue.
They fear what they might lose.

Such is the case in South Africa. It has been a primitive
country in a pre-civil war situation for years. It's basically
functioning on the level of the American 1860s. It was inevitable that those who were in victim roles would take
action. The white leadership must move into the Balanced
Big Picture or people will continue to die for the principle
of equality. Our own national history is filled with that
lesson.

*"I do believe we all can become better than
we are, but the price is enormous and we aren't
yet willing to pay it."*
James Baldwin,
Contemporary American
Writer

Each of us must, ultimately, face the larger order of
brotherhood and respectful relationships. Decreased dependent attachments, increased self-awareness and connected respect for others will bring responsible behavior.
In each person's lifetime, many such deep recovery opportunities present themselves.

The Lone Ranger and Helpless Victim defensive patterns have addictive, repetitive lives of their own. They are, in the short run, self-supportive and breed their own gratification circle. For a while, they seem to work and do provide a temporary measure of comfort. There are *apparent* gains to be had by manipulating or controlling others. But they don't last over time.

As medical director of a large and very successful inpatient chemical dependency, relationship dependency, and eating disorder program, I see these patterns everyday. Behind every chemical addiction is a psychological dependency problem. Behind every psychiatric hospitalization is an unbalanced dependency pattern. And the psychological dependency problem can be most easily seen by taking a good look at the person's most intimate relationships. The closer people are emotionally, the more they are at risk and the more their defensive patterns reveal themselves.

Associated with every addictive disorder of any kind is a psychological dependency pattern. Peel away the gratification and with each new reality out jumps a Lone Ranger or Helpless Victim. Every "codependent" relationship is based on emotional dependency. Every addictive disorder, besides being comfort-driven, is only an attempt to cover the fear, the loneliness and the pain that we feel we shouldn't be having. Even the hard-core Lone Rangers will recognize and admit this fact when they realize they don't have to completely convert to victimhood to get well.

These dependency problems and defensive patterns are only superficially gender-related. As previously mentioned, many women are profound Lone Rangers, and many men are pitiful Helpless Victims. In recent history, men's and women's roles have changed. But all have the same elemental problems. We were all programmed from our childhood and back from the Stone Age. Our defensive patterns don't vary by sex, and they don't vary by religion or race. They are expressions of the human mind working against the natural order. They are the defensive patterns of our upline parents all the way back to 400,000 years ago. They are corporate, they are national, they are personal and private. They are the issues that leaders and their followers live and die by. They are the basis for most human suffering.

If we can just see the patterns — how we dodge and weave through relationship realities seeking our own illusions — perhaps we can overcome them.

> *It is thus, if there is any rule, that we ought to die — neither as victim nor as fanatic, but as the seafarer who can greet with an equal eye the deep that he is entering, and the shore that he must leave.*
>
> *Edward Morgan Forster*
> *English Novelist*

6

Your Unbalanced Childhood:

How It Affects Your Adult Life

Every man has his own Annapurna.
    Sir Edmund Hillary, Mountain Climber

NATURAL PATTERNS OF CHANGE existed long before the dawn of recorded history. Scholars in both ancient and contemporary cultures have recognized these patterns and, in fact, have written extensively about them. It is our charge to understand these cycles, accept that they exist independently of human struggles, and to live creative lives in harmony with them. But even as we begin to understand them and see their relevance, we must face yet another task — we must overcome the patterned, defensive illusions of our childhood.

Our defensive pattern of limited reductionistic thinking is intensified by our poor understanding of the use of language and by the limited perceptions of our immediate mentors. In relationships, such unbalanced, short-sighted viewpoints encourage the persistence of childhood illusion patterns and make us unhappy, angry and disappointed. And it is these very defenses that lead people to drug addiction, suicide, murder, divorce, civil war, and even world war. Reductionistic, diacritic thought patterns keep us out of touch with universal reality, the patterns of change and the Natural Order.

In the Himalayan mountains, there are many majestic and awe-inspiring peaks. Each has its own mystery and foreboding grandeur — each its own difficult paths. If you are to see the world, you must trek up your own mountain. You must leave your childhood paths and seek your own way through the high talus and the snow.

Our immediate mentors have taught us to manipulate reality — not learn from it. With every technological advancement comes greater expectations of increasing comfort and decreasing responsibility. These expectations keep us from seeing that we each must climb our own Annapurna — our own wild mountain of limited perceptions. Each of us does have an opportunity to climb that personal relationship mountain of self-discovery. But, our childhoods leave us with limited perceptions about our relationships.

If we seek that self-discovery outside of ourselves, we will be left feeling empty and disappointed. The mountains seem too high — the journey too painful. We have accepted the fallacy that if we change the world, we will change ourselves. Now, we must accept the paradox that the only way to change the world is to change ourselves and our perceptions — to take fundamental responsibility for our own lessons. We *can't* change others, but we *can* change ourselves.

Looking more inside ourselves, we may seek to affirm or disprove our parents' view of us as children. Whole lives are spent in attempts to prove our mothers and fathers right or wrong. But such lives are limited by the parameters of previous generations — limited by their choices and their awareness.

There is, reportedly, a sign by a dusty road outside of Patagonia, Arizona. It says, "Choose with care the rut you drive in; you'll be in it the next 40 miles." Your childhood relationship defensive patterns are also chosen, and they are some of the most difficult defensive patterns to overcome. I remember a young man whom I saw in family therapy with his parents. His predominant energy focused on disproving his father. He argued categorically and defended categorically. "Always," "never," "all," "every" and "only" were his favorite words. When he couldn't make a case that his father was saying these words against him, he was using them against his father. "You mean you think I *only* ...?" "You mean you *never* did that when you were a kid?" He was a categorical traveler, trapped in that 40-mile rut. He sought to control others, while his father controlled him.

Ann Smith, author of *Grandchildren of Alcoholics,* has clearly shown how the psychological dependency patterns in alcoholic homes can be passed down and result in similar patterns generations down the line. Others have reported interesting studies on such issues as intergenerational grief. These studies show, for example, how some Jews who experienced the trauma of the Holocaust, developed constricted, dependency-forming life patterns that passed unrecognized through their own children only to surface as compulsive overeating disorders in grandchildren with unresolved grief issues.

Directly facing and understanding your unbalanced past will help with recovery and provide valuable lessons for your journey up the mountain. But at the outset, let me raise a word of caution. The past will provide only *some* answers — not all of them. Some people get locked in treatment — stuck because they can't remember or can't see the trauma in their past. They are frustrated and determined, as they work their memory screen to a frazzle. With dazed eyes and sleepless nights, they vainly seek details of the past. *But research has shown that the trauma may have been more than a generation ago.* It may be beyond memory. Still, effective treatment must include a review of the past. It must connect whatever yesterday is available with your today, so that you can take *corrective action.* Review you parents' fears, control and avoidance. Review their unbalanced patterns. These patterns can teach you about yourself.

Another caution is that so much "therapeutic" remembering of the past seems to be predicated upon the goal of assigning blame and responsibility for your current state of affairs. If you could just remember who did what to you and why it hurt so much, you could then name the villains. You could reject them, get angry with them, write virulent letters to them and thereby heal the wounds. But blame certainly doesn't work. Catharsis doesn't work, either.

Freud discovered that fact in 1892 when he gave up the use of hypnotic regression as a cathartic therapeutic tool. Of course, catharsis might make you feel better, but feeling better doesn't lead to self-discovery. Your past wounds must *connect* with your current experience — that is, with the way you are now living your daily life. This connection can occur by melding the past and present through psychoanalysis or by simply recognizing the transference or inheritance of past patterns in everyday life.

Put another way, your family patterns from childhood live on in the way you live your life today. Your daily relationships reflect the patterns of your childhood. Both balanced and unbalanced aspects of your relationship with your parents live on in your present relationships with spouses, employers and employees, friends and your own children. It is not at all surprising (and occurs quite often) that people in treatment come to the realization that they are behaving in exactly the way they themselves were treated by a parent. They have themselves become the tyrannical or helpless parent with whom they were so angry.

Most of us don't wish to make this essential connection. But the fact is that control issues *are* relentlessly passed on in either active control (LR) or passive control (HV) forms. Those control and avoidance patterns are ultimately self-destructive. Such patterns are often based on the parents' perception of reality. If parents fear some aspects of reality, and seek to avoid or control it, they pass that means of coping onto their offspring.

The fact that our parents' defensive patterns impact us is irrefutable. Exactly *how* they affect us requires more precise individual scrutiny. For example, if one of your parents was a LR and the other was a HV, then you would have been raised with conflicting defensive patterns, and it would be likely that your adult patterns would also be mixed. On the other hand, two LR parents will, most likely, raise a LR child, and two HV parents will frequently raise a HV child. Sometimes patterns of coping skip generations. At other times, they produce the reverse of what might be expected.

That is, avoidant and permissive victim parents may encourage the development of LR children, while LR parents may encourage an overtly passive, victim-oriented child.

That brings to mind a woman I once treated. Her victim-patterned parents lived in a commune, wore combat boots and fatigue jackets, and practiced open marriage. They smoked marijuana and didn't bathe often. They had diffuse boundaries. The patient, on the other hand, always appeared for therapy sessions remarkably beautiful and immaculately dressed. She reacted to their poor self-management and victimhood by excessive self-control. Her boundaries were profound and obvious. She looked, at nearly 30 years old, like a cover girl for *Seventeen* Magazine. Her defenses crystallized into a pattern opposite that of her parents. She was determined to never become a victim.

Your childhood patterns must be understood and resolved to some degree. How can you free yourself to make a larger order contribution to the development of society if you're still angry or hurt with your father or mother? You *must* grapple with your childhood patterns in order to free yourself and find balance in recovery. You must free yourself from the inaccurate perceptions and fears of your family, and forgive your parents for what they didn't know and couldn't do. You aren't your mother or your father. Your life can't be lived *now,* if you're caught back then.

I had an interesting experience with a gentleman I had been seeing in group therapy for almost two years. He had always been a serious LR in group — quiet, reticent, judgmental and distrustful. Yet in love relationships, he was a HV, asking often for his partner's guidance. One day, he came to group particularly reticent and looking sad. He quietly sat down, looking like someone had beaten him with a stick. When I asked if he was alright, he said, "Sure." When I pried more and asked if there was a problem, he emphatically said, "No." I continued asking questions in an effort to engage him in conversation, but he resolutely maintained that there was no problem. Finally, his reluctance abated, and he confided to the group that his father had died a week earlier. He fought back tears, but he continued to maintain, "No problem. Another funeral, that's all."

Only later did I discover the reason for his evasive reaction. As a child, he had been terrorized by his alcoholic father and had often been beaten in public — a secret he had kept through two years of therapy. He had not revealed this fact because he "thought the past was unimportant." For over 50 years, he had tried vainly to make it insignificant.

Let me be emphatic on this point: Your past pain must be understood. Your past experiences and your reactions to them are your only lessons for the present and future. The goal is not simply to put them behind you, but to recognize and accept the lessons they offer. Learn to recognize and correct your own misperceptions and accept the accurate ones. Forgive, but don't forget. Recognize their patterns and your reaction to them.

All your "merit badge" accomplishments in life — from childhood trophies to "employee of year" — can only give you glimpses of your true abilities. Such accomplishments can actually be a liability if you fall back on them as a solace for today's confusion. Good times and achievements can show you where you may have been in balance, but they can also betray you into feeling sorry for yourself. They can distract you from the difficult and painful path of facing your today. Your childhood pain and rejection, the feelings of being misunderstood, are serious training for climbing the mountains of daily life. In exploring the difficulties of your past, you will be able to pinpoint the origins of your current repetitive patterns.

CHILDHOOD PAIN

First of all, let's get firmly past the blame part. Even if your parents were *conscious* of what they were doing, they didn't really *know* what they were doing. The psychology of children, their perceptions of the world and the fact that childhood events matter at all — these are only recent discoveries.

Let's assume that our parents didn't understand what they were doing, even if *they* think they did. They tried to teach us "the only way they knew." They tried to teach us about reality *"as they perceived it."* That's it. No more, no less. And they taught us about that reality with an *emotional force* of control based on *their own fears and insecurities*. They often didn't see the Big Picture, but they taught us the basics about not walking in the street to avoid cars and staying out of mud puddles to avoid polio. My father's only advice about sexual activity was, "If it rains, remember to wear your rubbers." Weeks later, I realized he was talking about sex. I certainly don't blame him for his abbreviated remarks. He probably heard even less from his father. At least, he did take a stab at it. And, of course, from his perspective, I may not have wanted to *hear* it from him at that time, anyway. I may not have been ready for the lesson. In interesting contrast was the remark made by my 13-year-old son while our family was traveling on a vacation in the West. The subject of prophylactics had come up, and we began to talk about the different types. He asked me if I knew that "the AIDS virus could be transferred across the membrane of a lambskin prophylactic." The questions and times have surely changed. I truly appreciated his junior high sex education course, and I was duly surprised at the source of this new information regarding sex. On this occasion, both students were ready.

Our parents gave us, as best they could, the basics of how we could get hurt by aspects of reality — but no Big Picture. No relationship lesson plan. It wasn't their fault. They may have given us occasional paddlings for various transgressions. The pain was meant to indicate "don't do that again." But how do we master those passive situations that caused us pain as children? The answer is that we actively *repeat* them.

Think about it. If children go to the dentist and have their teeth drilled on all afternoon, they experience pain from a passive/receiver position. If we carefully watch those children, they are apt to go home from the dentist and pick up their dolls to play dentist themselves. By drilling away on a doll, *they turn a passive experience into its active counterpart in an effort to master the previous fears.*

Adolf Hitler, the son of an angry alcoholic, tried to bully the entire world. He thought he was right, and the world was wrong. He was out of balance.

The same reasoning explains why some women who have been sexually molested as children become prostitutes, or why it is that some kids at school are bullies — they've been bullied at home. Children grow up blindly and regularly repeat their traumatic childhood experience in an effort to master that same experience. The little girl was previously frightened. Now she's in the driver's seat. The boy was frightened. Now he's the boss. Our adult lives are manipulated, controlled, externalized manifestations of frightened, internal childhood experiences. We try to control the world to manage our fears, and many lifetimes are wasted as a result. Patterns of control and self-victimization form a connected web of intergenerational hurting and being hurt that lasts until we die — or until we begin to look for the Big Picture. Of course, there are childhood traumas less obvious than neglect and abuse. An ancient Chinese proverb compares the difficulty of raising children to flying a kite. Parental control should move with the developmental winds of change and the child's perceptions of reality. If parents pull children too hard into the wind, they go down. If parents let go too quickly, again the children go down. Parents can either overprotect or underprotect their children. They can be too overprotective by standing between the child and natural consequences, or too harsh by regularly presenting their own unbalanced perceptions through neglect, rage, "love," disrespect, sarcasm or other inappropriate manipulations.

LOVE AND CONTROL

The least obvious "trauma" of childhood is too much control through "love." I've heard it said, "He was such a good boy. How did he go so bad?" "She came from such a good family. How could she have died of a heroin overdose?" "His family loved him so much. Why did he kill himself over a single "B" the first year in college?" The answer: they were "loved" too much.

Love can kill you as surely as heroin, and "love" problems from childhood can have disastrous consequences in adult life. Confused? Perhaps if I use some words other than "love," you can begin to see some of the problems more clearly. Try thinking in terms of "permission," "need," "want," "require," "wish" and "demand." Statistics tell us that at least 80 percent of homicides are "domestic incidents." And how many people have committed suicide for love? Who knows? But lovers have died for each other since time immemorial. And people are still *flattered* to hear their lovers say, "I love you ... I need you ... I can't live without you ... I would die for you." Think of how many contemporary songs have as their main theme, "I need you."

This, my friends, is primitive thinking! "I need you." That's what cavemen said to each other. Do you really want to go into a relationship because you're an external answer to someone else's needs? Do you want him or her to rely on you for permission to live and achieve? Do you want to be as a drug or food to another person? Do you *want* a parasitic relationship in which the other person sucks you up and uses you for his needs?

Now, you may think you can find a mate because, after all, "you have needs, too." But then you, too, become a parasite — a parasite on a parasite. You become a user. Your partner becomes your fix against the cycles of nature and the changes of the universe. Intellectually, we know everything occurs in cycles, but still we believe change won't happen this time. Our defenses operate like musical chairs. We're afraid we'll be left without the chair if we don't tie ourselves to it umbilically and parasitically. And, just as tying ourselves to the chair is limiting, too much love is limiting. Too much love/need becomes an obsession. Obsessions obviously limit choices, and such limited relationships preclude balanced life action. I again suggest we eliminate the emphasis on *needs* and recognize our *choices*.

TOO MUCH LOVE

Being "loved" too much in childhood is just as dangerous as not being loved enough. "Love" may be synonymous with "overprotection." Moreover, parents may find themselves in a fatal attraction with their children and may sacrifice their entire lives for the demanding fledglings. It's been my ob-

servation that our prisons are filled with those who have
been loved too much. Their loving parents protected them
far too long from the vagaries of the passing scene. They
controlled them and kept them close. They fretted over
them and worried about their futures. They trapped them
in the family, in the home and in the love-dependency
system.

One of the most difficult, hard-core heroin addicts I've
worked with had several tours in chemical dependency re-
habilitation centers. He's served several years in the state
prison for armed robbery, as well. Yet, he kept relapsing
with heroin. In spite of a positive treatment situation, he
seemed to slide backwards. The man was angry. He was
mean. But I accidentally discovered an important piece in
the puzzle before his last departure from the hospital. This
man received loving calls from his dear mother every day,
wherever he was. And, that's not all. She smuggled marijuana to him in a birthday cake while he was in prison. He
was *loved* into a box. The box his mother created for him
became a prison cell that fueled his heroin addiction. Before
it's over, her love may be his coffin.

This counterdependent, heroin addicted, ex-con was trying to break *away* from his mother's smothering love.
Permissive parental love sets no boundaries, so children feel
entitled to do as they please. That's why they behave badly.
They are saying, "Don't love me so much — I can't stand it."
At the same time they seek out people who will enable them
and permit their behavior, they beg for structure. They
want self-respect. They want someone strong enough to be
consistent with the rules. And what they really want is the
chance to develop the internal discipline to run their own
lives. But because they are fighting *against* the control
prison of love, they can't trust and, in fact, express rage at
anything that's loving. They are afraid that love might
make them weak and that they might again be manipulated or victimized by it. Bottom line — they *don't want to
be manipulated.* And what are they experts at?
Manipulation. They relentlessly try to manipulate the
world to avoid being manipulated, because they have been
manipulated so much at home.

ENTITLEMENT

The urge to manipulate is motivated by a feeling of entitlement. If you carry the pain of a childhood hurt or trauma, how do you feel? Special. You think your pain is special. No one has had it quite like you. And because you feel *special,* you also feel *entitled.* You may think, "Anyone who has suffered as much as I have, has a right to have it the way they want it."

If you've been *lovingly overprotected* in your childhood, and haven't had to deal with the real world, how do you feel? Special. You've been loved in a *special* way. And since you had it that way in your childhood, you think you're *entitled* to have it that way in your adult life. Just what is it that you are entitled to? To have your *needs* met. Of course! If you've been loved too much or not enough, you feel entitled. And, how many of us have not been loved too much or not enough?

Moreover, the sense of entitlement can become compounded by the American way of life. We're free people. So, therefore, we assume that we're *entitled* to do what we want. Instead of seeking appropriate rights, we demand privilege. Someone will pay for our pain. We will no longer be victims. Whole countries or groups of people can, just as individuals, come back from a role of national victimhood to one of excessive power and control.

The expectations of entitlement fill jails and prisons. It is the nadir of Lone Ranger expectancy. It disregards boundaries, social position and the helplessness of others. Often, it is associated with other addictions or chemical dependencies, sexual privilege and "power." It can be found from the pimp on the street to the CEO in the boardroom.

Some professionals and celebrities feel entitled. They think that because they have paid their dues, they can behave disrespectfully. I knew a young physician in residency training. He was bright and obviously knew it. During clinical case presentations, he would make jokes about the material being presented. Puns, plays-on-words, sarcasm and put-downs were a part of his regular routine. Often, the absent patient being discussed was the butt of his jokes.

One day, the group was led by a wise, old Jewish doctor who had the bearing and presence of a Talmudic scholar. After the resident made a particularly inappropriate remark during one case presentation, the supervisor turned thoughtfully to him and said, "Doctor, you've been through high school, college, medical school and internship — many years of education. Now here you are, your second year in residency and ... no one has bothered to call you a shmuck."

The observation certainly hit the mark. His intelligence and entitlement had set him up. The resident thought all along that his observations were special. He clearly had a measure of childhood programming. He was special. It was only a matter of time until someone sat on him.

Lone Ranger entitlement is a dependency, a dependency on victims and fear. It attracts the weak and insecure, the parasites and the groupies of the world. It is a fear of dependency, manifested in denial. On the other hand, Helpless Victims feel entitled to be taken care of — to have others take care of life for them. Both demonstrate the victim process of manipulation through "love." Remember: Entitlement takes.

Conversely, traumas or loving overprotection during childhood can also leave people feeling the reverse: that they aren't worthy of anything. Either they never had love and don't feel they deserve it, or they had it so good that they know it will never be that good in adult life. Their perceptions, through hurt and overprotection, are turned into helpless surrender. The guilt overwhelms them. Their built-in sense of responsibility for others leads them to the conclusion that they are wrong and others are right. If, in childhood, they surrender to parental control patterns, they vow, as adults, never to be as selfish as their parents were. They flip into victimhood surrender and don't feel worthy enough to set boundaries with others to prevent their own pain. They often feel they can manipulate the world with love and kindness, so they refuse to become angry. They are overwhelmed by the fact that they can't change others through love, that they couldn't change their parents, and that they can't change their peers. They "die" developmentally because of their guilt. Someone back in their childhood had been suffering, and they became the caretaker, the bearer of the other's pain.

LOVE AND GIVING

People can give love in paradoxical ways. True love can indeed be free of the ominous and troublesome aspects of need fulfillment. I treated a man whose life experience drove him very close to death by alcohol. He had been a helicopter pilot who flew with a friend on a Vietnam jungle mission. Surprise enemy fire took their chopper into a crash landing. Fearing that incoming tracers would ignite the jet fuel, the pilot started to scramble out of the aircraft. But his partner couldn't budge. His legs were caught between the seat and the forward control panel.

Many pilots agree that the worst way to die is in flames, and it's their common fear. As his friend tried to free his legs, more tracers came in, and my patient fired several shots of protective cover with his pistol. He was forced to make a difficult choice quickly: to stay and die in flames himself, or leave his friend to die in flames.

In an act of kindness and love, my patient killed his friend. As he jumped from the chopper, it exploded. He had been drinking ever since to deaden the pain of having loved his friend in that way. When he was able to see the shooting as an act of love, he began to heal. But previously, when he had only seen it as a hostile act of killing, he tried to kill himself with alcohol.

Killing his friend in that situation was a selfless act in that it fulfilled none of his own needs. But he was caught in a categorical trap — unable to come to grips with what was a positively motivated, compassionate, loving and yet, nevertheless, destructive act. He had no perception of the relationship field he shared with his friend. His action was a lesson in friendship. It was unselfish. Love doesn't always come in conventional packaging. His own childhood had been characterized by enormous feelings of guilt and responsibility for his alcoholic mother.

CULTS AND SATANISM

We can't leave the discussion of childhood without briefly reviewing some groups our own children might join. And we must start with the positive rather than the negative. What do love cults and satanic practice offer an adolescent or young adult? What's the *positive* aspect of joining such a group? Well, each group offers two different and separate *need-fulfilling opportunities.* Groups such as the Moonies offer an illusion of perfect love and protection that is ideal for HV's. If the child felt unloved, he might join because he feels entitled to be loved. If the child felt overly loved and special, joining a love cult might be a perfect resolution to fears of leaving home and going out into the cruel world, perceived reductionistically and addictively as negative. Cults and other fundamentalist groups may say, "We're all good and love. The world is negative." They preach categorical thinking because they haven't seen the value of growing through understanding one's self and one's own difficulties. To them, difficulties are negative experiences from which the group offers safety. They depend on the patterns of fear and control that are already present within their prospective candidates.

Satanic cults are at the other end of the love/hate spectrum. Patricia Pulling, author of *The Devil's Web,* a study of satanism and the occult, presents an important positive dimension to joining a satanic order. Many satanic worshipers are there because they are seeking freedom. They want no rules. They want to do what they want to do. No manipulation! They have rights, etc. What are they against? Love! They revile love traps including respectful sex, intimacy and caring, all of which they see as weak. A satanic cult is a serious LR place to go. If you're tired of being manipulated into caring for someone else, why not go all out, take complete and selfish care of yourself, and take advantage of others. Satanism is a place to be free of guilt, a ready spot for fascism, sexual license and racism. Who wants to take care of anyone else? Satanists want freedom from love's guilt and control. The satanic order gives them an illusion of freedom from provocative guilt and responsibility for others. They can hate without reserve.

If you look closely around at the groups and clubs you belong to and the values they encourage, I wouldn't be surprised if you find certain fundamentalist aspects. How many corporate, vertical-thinking, self-made Lone Ranger bosses seek complete and selfish control to avoid being loved "that way" again. How many HV's go to therapists and support groups, remain dependent on their advice, comfort, and support, and yet don't take specific corrective action to fully live their own lives? The patterns are there from childhood. Adult life is a manifestation of childhood programming. Through the unbalanced parental control they experience, adults fail to encourage the development of self-esteem in their own children. And if the present generation resists their loving parents by being selfish, *their* kids will be all too loving, the next kids will be all too selfish, and so on. The unbalanced cycle goes on through generations until someone connects with reality and, in recovery, begins to seek personal balance.

In summary, your areas of imbalance parallel those of your parents. Your defenses are based on their low self-esteem and their small-mind view of the world:

1. If they were too controlling, negative or judgmental, you could identify with those defenses and copy them, becoming an LR yourself. Or, you could work at avoiding those defenses and, in seeking to be "nice," could swing to the HV side and accept their view that you're defective.

2. If your parents were weak and dependent, you could identify with their fears and dependency and manifest HV patterns in your relationships. Or, you could resent their defenses, caretake them and become a LR counter-dependent.

3. Most of us, to some degree, regularly run the perceptual tapes that our parents have given us about ourselves. We accept their perceptions of reality in other areas, so why not regarding our own "shortcomings"? Their perceptions become our belief systems, our values and our view of ourselves until our true self either accepts them as correct or rejects as incorrect, impractical and dangerous.

Your family, your job, your club, your marriage and your other relationships can't make you either special or worthless. They can't take you up your difficult mountain. As you discover yourself, you will gradually shed the unbalanced relationship misperceptions passed on by others. Over time, you will come to see the defensive patterns used unsuccessfully by yourself and others in different kinds of group or individual relationships. Through your increasing understanding of how the world works, you will be less likely to victimize yourself at the hands of others and less likely to paint yourself into a corner. *Your most meaningful relationships will become the key to your own personal balance and growth.* And as you begin to manage difficulties better, you will further confirm your Big Picture awareness and understanding and become more confident in your practice. Your awareness and practice of correct action will take you higher up the central mountain. You will discover that *you have to climb the mountain yourself.* You must overcome what your parents have told you about their biases and fears. If they were controlling or avoidant, your adult relationship experience will show you their pain. The more you climb, the more you will see the climb that everyone must make. Leaving the defensive patterns of your parents will help you find your own freedom from patterns. Whether you parents are alive or dead, you must resolve your conflicts with them and practice respectful self-protection. Unresolved conflicts with parents perpetuate ongoing relationship difficulties in other aspects of your current life.

Leaving those childhood illusions will teach you about each next step and the choices you must make. You will learn when you're using old patterns to cope because they will cause pain. If you give in and listen too much, or argue, you're the one with the problem. It's easy, at times, to continue the patterns because they are expected by your parents. Unthinking, defensive repetition will tempt you, but with fresh relationship choices in your current life, you will grow into new relationship opportunities. You can change your relationship with your parents as well. Balance must be present in every adult relationship or you will fall out of recovery.

You will ultimately discover, up on the mountain, that you never forget the painful lessons of your unbalanced childhood patterns. The resolution of these patterns will keep you on the mountain path of your adult life.

7

Self-Esteem —
To Be Or Not To Be:

Choice As The Path To Your Self

"To be or not to be that is the question — whether it is nobler in the mind to suffer the slings and arrows of outrageous fortune or to take arms against a sea of troubles and by opposing end them."
William Shakespeare

HAMLET'S QUESTION IS ONE WE ALL ASK OURSELVES. What to do? Sit back and passively accept reality as it comes, or get up and address the reality head-on? To be or not to be? What do I do with myself? It's the ultimate self-esteem question — the same metaphoric question that Robert Frost asks himself in the woods: "Two roads diverged in a yellow wood and *sorry I could not be one traveler and travel both* long I stood ..." We'd prefer not to choose. We want to have our cake and eat it, too. We would like to be "one traveler and travel both (paths)."

But if we care about our own development, we must begin to make choices. Choice is an action that moves you to a different reality. Decisions keep you in tune with the changing universe. Now that we are beginning to see the Big Picture better, we are more aware of the dangers and pain associated with not facing reality. We know that we must start to face relationship realities and walk up the mountain. Choices become manifest through specific actions.

CHOICES

Up to this point, our discussion has been like a flashlight on a darkened trail. The light of these words has allowed you a faint glimpse of reality and the Big Picture. But, only by the process of actually taking action and walking up that trail can you see the natural light that presents itself through relationship choice-making. The illuminating process of growth begins and ends with choices and the natural change that results from them. To avoid making choices can only result in stasis and boredom, a living death. My advice to Hamlet would have been: to be *and* to choose. For in choosing, you will come to know your *self*.

Remember the two timeless admonitions chiseled on the Oracle of Delphi in ancient Greece: "Know Thyself" and "To Thine Own Self Be True." But, *before* you can know yourself, and *before* you can witness self-truth, you must decide upon an action and take it. You'll know if your choice is right for you, because you will feel right after you make it. Correct action builds on itself. Through relationship choice-making, you find out who you are. Inappropriate choice and action brings shame, which is not the same as guilt. Shame is an internal message that tells that you have done less with yourself than what was required by the situation.

It doesn't matter if anyone else knows. *You* know how you played it. Your own self will talk to you. Your cosmic horn will talk. You will know if you contribute to the higher order, to the development of humanity. You will know also if you take, if you hide or if you procrastinate, because avoidance brings pain. Every small decision helps you overcome the fear of change — change that is necessary to the growth process. In fact, by making a decision, you become the instrument of change within yourself. Over time, with many decisions, you will gradually see your own value system emerge. You will know which decisions give you a "right" feeling before and after the choice.

Furthermore, right choices are balanced and won't set you up. You won't victimize yourself through a lack of balance. Your "self" is, in fact, your value system. It's what you stand for. It's what you believe in. And with your emerging value system, you'll come to know when you kid yourself, when you quit, when you hang back too long and when you practice self-deception. What you stand for determines which actions to take and which to resist.

Let me take a slight exception with the Oracle. You will never *absolutely* "know yourself," because your perceptions of reality are changing regularly. But you can *begin* the process of knowing yourself. There is no arrival at a station of specific awareness down the line, no absolute knowledge. There is only the journey, the process of paying attention. When people won't choose to change or won't accept change, they have, in fact, made a choice — a single, final choice. It is a single decision, rather than many decisions, that reduces the reality variables and can result in subsequent self-destructive, repetitive actions. True choice prevents simple, primitive repetition and accepts the change process.

TIMING

It should be pointed out that not *acting* is not necessarily the same as not *choosing*. Choice is not always associated with overt action. It sometimes waits for the appropriate time to present itself. You can victimize yourself by too much choice and action, or by too little. If you wait too long to make your choice, you will become a victim. Reality will relentlessly force you to the decision, and you will fight the natural order of change. On the other hand, too many actions are an effort to manipulate and push the timing of the natural order. Nature will strike back.

"God, grant me the serenity to accept the things I cannot change, the courage to change the things I can, and the wisdom to know the difference."
Reinhold Niebuhr
The Serenity Prayer

Let's look at the words of this well-known prayer, line by line. "Grant me the serenity to (choose to) *accept* the things I cannot change." This phrase is a request for help to stay out of Lone Ranger control patterns and a reminder to remain respectful. There are people and situations that are beyond our control. We can't control many aspects of most relationships. There are many natural events we cannot change. We must develop respect for the natural order and lay aside our ego, our cognitive explanations. We can't ignore the fact that some people simply don't agree with us.

The prayer continues with "... the courage to (choose to) *change* the things I can." This is a request for strength to *decide* and *act,* to abandon a passive Helpless Victim role. Because avoidance doesn't work, either. It addresses the fear we all have of natural change. We need courage to choose for ourselves and to face the prospect of the new responsibilities that come with new choices and new action. Having the courage to change things is self-protective and refutes a caretakee position.

Next, we need "... the wisdom to know the difference." As we *choose* to accept or manage the realities that come our way, we will become wiser in time. Through wisdom, we will find balance with relationships and with nature. We will remain free of excessive active control or passive inaction, and we will be able to see more and more of the Big Picture. Wisdom builds further recovery.

All the new evidence in neurolinguistic programming indicates that we frame our lives up. We lock in unconsciously and cruise through life with blindfolds on. Often, we don't even know we're cruising. On an unconscious glide path through reality, we don't care to see the trees.

Recently, I rented a car while visiting my daughter at her summer camp south of Ashville, North Carolina. The steering in the rental car was different from that of my own car, and the roads were mountainous with hairpin turns. I was faced with two new variables of reality — the steering and the roads. Nevertheless, I continued to drive automatically as I would at home in my own car. The result was that I went off the road slightly several times. Finally, I realized I had to *think* about the *road* and think about the *steering*. I had to *connect* with those new realities.

In neurolinguistic programming research, it's been found that even a small change can make a difference. The smallest awareness within the choice process can alter your behavioral patterns. For example, think about the first time you moved, joined a gym or went for a long run. Each was a new reality with different variables. Making the choice to connect and seek the developmental way — to *explore* new realities, even in your own backyard — will free you from cruising blindly.

Some people retire and are happier than ever. Others can't find anything to do. Their identity was in their work, so they can't enjoy retirement. Malcolm Forbes said it well: "The hardest job is no job at all." People like this can't accept change.

Sadly, I've known several people who committed suicide when their mates died. Their identity had been dependent upon a single person. They couldn't adapt to the change of their loved one being gone. And in a somewhat less drastic situation, how many people refuse to enter a new relationship once they've been hurt in love? They don't want to risk the pain. "I'll never fall in love again," goes the familiar song.

If you decide to *not decide*, thereby putting off the decision process, it means you're struggling to maintain control. You fear the moment of change and the new variables you'll encounter, because each decision invites a new and different responsibility. At that moment of non-decision, you freeze and victimize yourself by stepping out of the natural change that's going on around you. Remember that phrase "... the courage to change the things I can." By not deciding, you're sticking with what you think you know and avoiding what you don't know. But the natural order of change, once understood, is actually more consistent than our frail attempts to control things.

The unseen design of things is more harmonious than the seen".

Heraclitus, 500 B.C.,
Greek philosopher

It's easier to float in a tube down life's river of change than to swim against the current. Floating is easier than grabbing wildly at attachments — to jobs, relationships, "love" or mind-altering chemicals. If you accept the fundamental naturalness of change, there will always be new job opportunities and something to choose to do the next moment. With this new awareness, you'll always have a job — your life. But without it, you'll often become bored. Life will feel meaningless. Yours will be a mad, Jack Kerouac search out there on the road. And, as singer Jackson Browne said, You'll be "running against the wind."

By actually making choices, you will see very clearly where your attachments are. You'll begin to see how you hang on to old ways and to the ample distractions that keep you from your life's work. Codependency literature has a great term: "external referenting." It means to take your meaning (referent) from outside reality. Your status, your social position and your "power" can all be seductions based upon seeking approval. Through choice, you'll soon come to see where your values are caught up in what others think about you. And each time you base a decision on seeking approval through external referenting, you'll be untrue to yourself. And, being true to yourself isn't selfish — it's responsible. The more responsible you are with yourself, the more likely that others around you will be responsible with themselves.

A friend once inquired if Gandhi's aim in settling in the village and serving the villagers as best he could was purely humanitarian. Gandhi replied...
"I am here to serve no one else but myself, to find my own self-realization through the service of these village folk."
Robert Aitken, Zen Monk

Humanitarian service smacks of caretaking, but that's only one side of the exchange. Gandhi saw both sides. He was of service, but he also *received* understanding and enlightenment in return. He gave *to* them and he received *from* them. Through his choices and his actions, he came to see what his attachments were within that village. No doubt, he learned from the village, and, of course, his actions were helpful to them. But he did not go to rescue anyone from their own self-realization, nor to impose his own self-realization upon them. He went there for the exchange — to share and receive at the villagers' level.

There may be those who want you to completely forget about yourself and just do for them. Naturally, it's important to give and do for others, but the doing can't be the thoughtless type that will keep them from taking action for themselves. Nor can it be the type of help that sets you up as the "expert." Your doing for others should not be designed to rescue from their reality, nor to encourage their avoidance of it. Otherwise, you'd actually be doing them a disservice by making them dependent upon you. In the end, they would resent your caretaking mind-set.

TEACHING

Caretakers take away responsibility. Teachers, on the other hand, offer students the opportunity to try responsibility in a balanced way. Teachers don't protect students from reality or teach them avoidance. In showing others how to learn from reality, they, in turn, learn from the students. Teachers do not misrepresent the journey as being either too difficult or too easy because they know it is different for each student, depending on their individual decisions. Teachers work to remain aligned with reality and the natural order of change and to be sensitive to the desire for safety attachments that we all have. Each student is at a different level of awareness and acceptance.

CHARISMA

Charisma is a pestilence. We have had, as a race, too much charisma and illusion. A true teacher speaks humbly by example: "I am like you. If I can do it, you can. And you can teach me in return." Charismatic teachers try to teach perfection and entitlement, avoidance and control. Teachers of avoidance and control (dictators), who see their power and play it to the crowd, are no longer teachers. They immediately show they are followers. They follow their fears. True humility shuns charisma.

I had lunch one day with an extremely erudite professor who's been reading and searching for years. He's a philosophy maven and a repository of information. He's also a doer. He had read Capra, done Indian sweat lodges, traveled to China, and was in the midst of planning a sabbatical to spend several months in a trappist monastery. In short, he was not your average guy, and we had a wonderful conversation at lunch.

Yet, I couldn't help noticing that his remarks about any modality of understanding were negative. "It's only a model," he would say. Each way we turned in conversation, each perspective we considered, he summarily dismissed without exploring it. To him, each adventure was a nihilistic illusion, each undertaking only a different, useless paradigm.

Now, he may be arguably correct from a *content* point of view; there are indeed many models for self-discovery. But his limited, negativistic, Lone Ranger perspective failed to change *how* he lived. His decisions and choices hadn't evolved, because his highly evolved and critical intellectual apparatus kept him from taking the reality hit. He was as a world class fighter who wouldn't get into the ring. His mind kept him critically away from true choice-making, as he played with different realities. Oh, he would alter his reality momentarily, but without taking any risk. But riding a bus through Brooklyn is not living in Brooklyn. Touring isn't living. And choice is more than an intellectual process.

At a recent national meeting, a Zen monk proclaimed that "A person who is a jerk before enlightenment, will be a jerk after enlightenment." I am no monk, but I couldn't disagree more. If a person only *perceives* the larger natural order, but does not responsibly *enter it* through changed behavior, then that person remains in an intellectual dream. The mind may have led to insight, but, unfortunately, people can cycle repetitively through insight just as they can recycle through other attachments. Insight can serve as an avoidance of choices. It can be a safe place out of the natural order ... another trap, another tour. Recovery is more comprehensive than psychotherapy, more active than psycho-analysis and more responsible than insight.

In this journey, whatever mode of reality you use to reveal your true self to yourself — whether it's work, sports, the arts or relationships — you must be disciplined and serious about bringing *your self* along. You must pay attention. That professor may well have been charismatic to his students. Charisma might have resulted because he could ostensibly set himself apart from the lessons. He appeared to be objective and above models. He saw no point in them. He was jaded, negative and a bit sarcastic. His intellectual experience was diverse, but he was filled with his own ego. He could not accept the lessons of his life because his cup was already filled with his own defensiveness.

Charismatic leaders attract groupies — those people who want to bask in the power of their idol's apparent perfection and "profound" awareness. Larger-than-life people who project perfect images are exceedingly loved by some and exceedingly reviled by others.

Think of the celebrities who have paranoid fans pursuing them. The fans may want them sexually, or they may want to take their "power" by hurting or killing them. Through sexual surrender to the groupie, gurus fall from grace. Gary Hart, Jim Bakker and Jimmy Swaggart all fell into the hands of groupies, some of whom have built large fortunes by taking those particular men down. These leaders had climbed the mountain to be fed, and they played to the crowd. The influence they had achieved was not used to teach the higher order, but as a means of self-gratification. A leader *is* in a more responsible position than the rest of us. They are in a position, through correct action, to advance our culture.

Film star Robert Redford once made an interesting remark regarding charisma and celebrity status:

> The bad part is that you become an object and there are three dangerous stages to that: One: People start treating you like an object. Two: You start behaving like an object. Three: You become one. That's terminal.

Leaders are drawn to be the people the crowd wants them to be. The crowd wants leaders who are perfect and who will love them perfectly. Yes, leadership *is* a difficult responsibility. The responsible leader assumes the larger commitment of being a significant influence over the lives of others. And therein lies an opportunity for the leader's own self-realization, lessons and personal growth. Leaders regularly have the opportunity, through leadership, to detach from the variety of seductions and attachments associated with the trappings of power. They have a greater opportunity to actually live in a different group reality. Leadership is a lesson opportunity for all of us. In even small groups, we can begin to stand up for values.

Yet, so often we see the difficult responsibility of leadership as a rationalization for unbalanced entitlement: "I worked so hard to get here." "I entertain you." "I work long hours for you." "I listen to your suffering." "Now, I want *you* to give *me* something back." The implication is apparent: "I worked hard so I could do what I want, break the rules and gratify myself without consequences. This is "celebrity entitlement": "I'm loved by many, so I can do whatever I want." The crowd's adoration of that apparent power encourages the denial of logical consequences. It presents a serious impediment in the chemical dependency treatment of entertainment people, physicians, lawyers and executives. They cannot see their underlying *psychological dependencies* because they are plugged with constant emotional fixes from the crowd. Because they are attractive, economically successful or intelligent, some people think they can avoid the realities of everyday life.

In order for such charismatic individuals to emotionally evolve, they must begin to break the denial that protects their own low self-esteem. They must face the new reality of responsible behavior. It's often hard for them to admit they're vulnerable — even five-percent vulnerable. And yet, if they can see the patterns of dependent vulnerability in their own lust for attention, love and appreciation, they can begin to heal.

Low self-esteem, the quest for acceptance, all of the addictions and relationship dependencies are psychologically

based on fear of the choices reality offers. The Helpless
Victims' fear is associated with a possible loss of love when a
choice is made. Someone might be offended. They might be
rejected or left alone. They might be a topic for gossip. But,
aren't we all often being talked about anyway? So what's
the difference? Make the higher order choice.

Lone Rangers do choose — but they choose to manipulate
and avoid, to remain disconnected. They choose compulsively and automatically without thought to the personal
sacrifices and losses or to the importance of relationships.
They fear the emotional pain associated with relationship
disputes.

THE HYDRAULIC THEORY

If dealing with all these repetitive dependency patterns
and attachments is confusing, let me introduce you to *The
Hydraulic Theory of Self-Esteem Regulation.* Think of all
the possible gratifications and safety stops as a closed hydraulic system. While being gratified by one, you're dis-
tracted from reality. Your self-esteem is protected. You don't
have to make any choices or risk making a mistake. But if
you choose to drop a specific gratification, and you've done
no work on your self-esteem, another springs up almost
hydraulically.

I once saw a medical student who was an alcoholic.
When he stopped drinking, he began gambling. This is a
very common situation. Most often, chemical dependency is
replaced by marked intensity in a dependent relationship.
The hydraulic self-esteem system regulates itself by seeking
from the outside world any support or distraction it can get.
Patterns of gratification are hydraulically interchangeable.
If a recovering patient's wife is furious and ends the marital
relationship while he's in the hospital, he will often attempt
to pair off sexually with someone else before he leaves the
program. If you're a celebrity and don't get gratification
from the crowd, perhaps you'll get it from chemicals or sex
— especially if you're hurt.

Knowing yourself and making your own choices unplugs
the whole hydraulic system. Self-esteem comes from inside,

from self-evaluation, rather than from the external hydraulic system. Your personal comfort system, your gratification and your way to feel good comes from the making of choices and the reality of a focused growth process. The process of choice-making brings about increasing self-awareness, decreased pain and diminished self-victimization.

Many people who don't see the larger order of this system are unenlightened and often loaded with non-decision attachment patterns. Such people create no problem unless they attempt to bring your decision-making process into their inability to make a decision.

I see this all the time in my practice. Once, I had a young, obviously bright attorney come in with the following agenda: "I will see you for two sessions. I will tell you everything I can about my wife. You will tell me at the end of those two hours if I should divorce her."

He clearly wasn't into self-discovery and he cared very little about understanding his wife except as to how he could manipulate her. He wanted to spend two hours working on his wife and no time on himself.

But, his decision had to be his decision. He only hesitated because he might hurt her, and he did feel guilty. But, he wasn't hesitating for reasons of a higher value system or for reasons of mutual respect. Nor did he choose to leave her because of her own failure to grow or develop from a restricted LR or HV pattern.

He left her in a "safe" way — with another woman. He was pumping along with his primitive hydraulic system bandaging his self-esteem by switching one person for another. He had to change gratifications, to find a new and better one. As B.B. King said, "The thrill was gone." The relationship, as a thrill and as a distraction, was no longer effective against his changing world.

In summary, here are some guidelines to keep in mind about choice:

1. Your victim roles force choice upon you.
2. If you are being victimized by non-recovering others, you must respectfully set appropriate boundaries. Choose your boundaries and choose your values. Hesitating to do so will create additional victimhood.

3. If you are victimizing yourself by *not* choosing to take action, you must be courageous and "change the things you can." A victim role is unbalanced non-recovery.
4. There are many who aren't seeking recovery and don't care about it. They are seeking control or avoidance. You seek your own true nature. *Choose* to structure or minimize your time with such people, because they work to pull you down to their level of denial.
5. When you are confused about how to set boundaries in complicted relationships, consistently practice respectful self-protection. Remain respectful of others' perceptions even though they differ from yours. Yet, remain firm on your boundaries and limitations with appropriate self-protection.
6. Compulsive choice-making (being picky) is a disrespectful longing for control.
7. Insufficient choice-making (being too "nice") is not self-protective and it seeks to avoid.
8. Choose to prioritize small choices as quickly as possible. Conversations with disrespectful, picky people can be ended early, yet courteously, because you accept early on that they don't desire change. Small choices made early eliminate difficult later choices.
9. Choose not to convert others to recovery principles. A regular effort to correct others is caretaking and disrespectful. They don't want to hear about codependency.
10. Entitlement and expectations are based on the assumption that you won't be forced to choose, that things will be taken care of for you.
11. Non-entitlement and having no expectations are based on the same assumption — that you won't be forced to choose and that things will be done for you.
12. Avoidance of reality and attempts to control it are ways of avoiding choice.
13. Choice is directly associated with a personal value system and self-esteem. Choice-making brings a sense of mastery and increases self-esteem.

14. "Wisdom to know the difference" implies having the wisdom to *choose* between the acceptance of things beyond your control and the courageous negotiation of win-win solutions in relationship situations that you previously avoided.
15. Each choice has a consequence. If you are a true student, that consequence is never a mistake, but rather a lesson to guide you in the next choice.
16. The fear of choice is the fear of being alone with the consequences. But the truth is that you are alone with or without the consequences. In recovery, you have your true self with you. That true self is aligned with the Natural Balance Order. Out of recovery, you have no connections with a spiritual path. Your only connections are your temporary relationship attachments.

EXPECTATIONS

Any diminished self-esteem system propels us through life, ever searching for metaphoric Band-Aids and avoiding choice. The associated "philosophy" is not the "Dead Poet Society's" *carpe diem* (seize the day), but rather seize the comfort, seize the safety. Many of us live our lives looking for privilege, entitlement, opportunities for denial and opportunities for power through which we can manipulate the world, so that it won't hurt us. And often, we simply can't see what we're doing. If we get married with big expectations, we are disappointed. If we take on new jobs with exaggerated expectations, we will surely find pain. Our great expectations, our entitlements, are our undoing.

In psychoanalytic training, I had an opportunity to work at the Philadelphia Association for Psychoanalysis with deep and gifted supervisor-mentors. As a student, I was filled with excitement and expectancy, in spite of the long and difficult training process. I felt, for the first time in my life, as though I could see solid answers to specific questions. With those answers, I could be trained to choose.

Then, a patient I had in analysis reported that she had tried to kill herself. She had loaded her husband's revolver with a single bullet and played Russian roulette. Not just once, either. She spun it again and pulled the trigger a second time. The third time she spun the cylinder, she paused and looked down the barrel. The bullet was in the chamber. She put the gun down and came in to tell me about it the next day.

I was shocked. I had known she was depressed, but she had seemed to be handling it. I flew back to Philadelphia for analytic supervision, full of expectations. I clearly needed some help in handling this difficult situation. I presented the problem to my analytic supervisor, who was a brilliant, experienced man. He slowly leaned back, sighed, and said simply, "This patient cannot be analyzed. Analysis is over. Supervision is over."

I was dumbstruck. I shuffled my papers a bit, mumbled a few more questions that went unanswered, gathered my things and left the office. I went back and continued treating my patient. I suggested she give me her guns for safe keeping, and they remained in my desk drawer for a year or so. Now, years later, she is happily married and functioning well. I see her in passing occasionally and she's most engaging and pleasant. She's alive with new activities. It was all a bad dream for her.

It was all a bad dream for me, as well. Her game of Russian roulette was another difficult initiation ceremony for me. Her situation unearthed my psychoanalytic illusion. Psychoanalysis had seemed limitless in its possible applications and usefulness. With such an advanced graduate level of study, I had thought I would be ready for whatever choices came up.

But in one respect, I had spent years of effort seeking a kind of haven in psychoanalysis. I had sought safety in insight. Analysis had become an attachment for me. That patient's gun booted me out of the nest of expectations and restated what I should have known already. I was on my own. That ediface of ideas had its own set of limitations. Deep insight leads to its own specific action.

That session with the supervisor was a profound lesson in my difficulty with expectations. I had believed that psychoanalysis could provide explanations for everything. Instead,

I found it could only explain some things. I was faced with the limitations of insight and the necessity for new choice and action.

The choices we make yield new opportunities for other choices. *The choice to think is not a choice of specific action.* A good factual education does not necessarily make one a good choice-maker. Remember the adage "overeducated and undertrained"? Education may, in fact, leave us with certain fixed belief systems from which we cannot detach ourselves.

As we grow beyond education, different ways of thinking offer new perceptions. As we choose new ways to think *and* subsequently behave, we attract new relationships and new choices. If we think, and subsequently behave, in ritualized, stereotyped patterns, we attract no new relationships, no new choices. We draw the same answers from the same believers.

Our relationships, such as my own with the supervisor and the patient, teach us where we are limited in our vision. Until we become aware of the larger order, we find that we often choose relationships that match and encourage our own limited vision. My valued relationship with the supervisor ended when the reality of my life changed and I was faced with new choices beyond his experience and conceptual framework. The patient's gun and the Russian roulette game were realities outside of his world that I was then forced to face. The supervisor's commitment to her treatment changed when the reality changed, but mine could not.

I was faced with a choice perplexity: Stay within a pattern of behavior and choice circumscribed by psychoanalysis, or seek a higher order and walk with the patient down that new road. Her new road was out there — beyond supervision and beyond analysis.

I was grateful, in the end, for a clean break and for a sharp slice across the illusions of what psychoanalysis could and could not do. Under the protective arm of my supervisors and my colleagues, I had found myself, on one level, expecting to be free from choices. But disappointments and expectations are always connected. My own expectations had led me, in a small way, to not think for myself. Each disappointment, however, is another opportunity to graduate up to a larger scale of perception. I was, at that moment in supervision, freed from my apparent security within psychoanalysis. That difficult moment provided the opportunity to work a different way — whatever way suited the patient, myself and the requirements of the treatment.

I was free to choose again in a new reality. Free, with a profusion of new questions. Free — to be or not to be.

8

Ongoing Recovery:

The Midnight Train
And The Rapids

Our life is the voyage of solitude.
A strong, true person, brave and great
Does not need help from others
Has no wish for it
We must become our true nature,
We must find our way into that true nature,
Walking firmly on the path
There is only my one self,
There is no second self beneath myself.
> *Taisen Deshimaru*
> *Zen Master, martial artist*

AFTER WE BEGIN TO SEE THAT THERE ARE CHOICES to make, we quickly begin to search for logical guidelines for making those choices.

Self-discovery is associated with the process of making choices throughout one's life. But how can we actually *learn* from our choices and make more of the right ones? How can we learn which choices will bring further self-discovery? The natural world order regularly gives us both choices and the opportunity for valuable lessons in a great variety of ways. But we can only see the lessons when our mind is prepared to accept them. Self-discovery requires constant mental preparedness for the lesson process.

Deep knowledge of the world order brings opportunity for self-discovery. Denial prevents you from recognizing the natural cycles in your own life. But after some ongoing self-study, you will make an important discovery. *You will learn that the painful, frozen, rusted places in your life are your friends.*

Your internal pain is your teacher. Your difficult relationships are your guide. Through troubled relationships, you can come to know your true self. There is an old Eastern saying: When the student is ready, the master appears. For many of us there have been no masters — only lessons that we couldn't understand. Masters discuss and reveal the larger order. But, *are* there any masters in Magnolia, North Carolina? Do you personally know any masters? Probably not. There are few masters and many relationships. And masters are human, too. They also have their limitations and can pass on their blinders to others.

Most of us are students of life. We are reflective, thoughtful and attempt to understand how this life works. Often, in later life, we do slowly begin to learn from our painful attachments. We belatedly become masters of our own fate. When we are ready, we *can* finally accept the lessons, which then become our teachers. *When the student is ready, the lesson appears.*

When we are young and full of ourselves, we are often busy reinventing the wheel. And so often that attitude can follow us throughout our lives. We believe in our own will, our ability to escape fate, and our power over others.

Lesson opportunities are wonderfully abundant and can occur through the simplest activities of daily life. Consider these hypothetical examples:

- Back in high school, a humorous Latin teacher jokingly called you "stupidisime stupidorum" (the stupidest of the stupid), meaning that you weren't perfect. How much grief could you have spared yourself had you accepted and understood that lesson back then?
- A job promotion you expected didn't materialize, and you weren't told why. This is a perfect opportunity for

you to review your work effort and your relationships with your peers and superiors. It is an opportunity for you to think about and plan your own future. It's not, after all, up to others to bring you along. Blaming them for your disappointments will only keep you from seeing yourself.
* Your first love dropped you at a critical moment in your life, and you were crushed. What you couldn't see at the time was that your loss was a metaphor. It revealed an idealization. The person you lost had his own limitations which you may have approached in an unbalanced way. Or, perhaps your loved one was too unbalanced for you, and you couldn't see it.

The lessons are there if you choose to see them. Your life need not be marred by severe tragedy. You don't need a special teacher, nor do you have to become a psychiatrist. The relationship lessons are everywhere, regardless of "family impairment." We write and sing about relationship lessons — we play with them in the media — but, we don't quite see them in our own daily lives. We don't live them. The student may feel ready, but the lessons remain out of reach. Pay attention — the lessons are there. Let's try an exercise. Think about the words of this song, and see if you can tell where the person is stuck.

L.A. grew too much for the man,
so he's leaving the life he's come to know.
He said he's going back to find
what's left of the world he left behind,
not so long ago.

He kept dreaming that someday he'd be the star
but he sure found out the hard way
that dreams don't always come true.

He brought a one way ticket back
to the life he once knew —
said he's going back to find
a simple place and time.
He's leaving, leaving
on that Midnight Train to Georgia.

"Midnight Train to Georgia"
Gladys Knight and the Pips

The answer is in that old saying, "You can never go home again." And when he goes home, he'll find out it has changed too. Home is itself an illusion of safety. The man in the song has pain. So, in his dark hour, he's heading back to safety and friends on the Midnight Train. He had a special life back there, one of safety and comfort — of apparent consistency. Out in L.A., he found there were too many new reality variables. He couldn't handle them, and so he was running home to the security of "known" variables.

Each of us has ridden our own personal Midnight Train. We've all sat alone on musty seats and watched the lights of life drift past in the darkness. We've all had our own blues and dark hours when we look inside for what went wrong. And face it, we've all longed to be somewhere safe where we won't have to feel that way again. What happens all too often is that we think a change in relationship geography will clear the air.

The man would do better to take the hit from reality and change his illusionary ways. Taking hits, accepting them and learning from his reality *could* make him the leader he wants to be. But his childhood denial program, his star search, led him to think that he just wouldn't have to work at it out in L.A. He was special. He was wonderful. Now, the opportunity is gone, and he's riding on a one way ticket back to a simple place and time.

It doesn't have to be that way. His dreams, his desires and his goals in life can all be realized if he sets them carefully and systematically in his mind and deals with each one every step along the way. Do you think he had an agent in L.A.? Do you think he had a demo tape? Was he prepared? It doesn't sound like it. He went out there with big dreams and no plan. He stuck out his chin and put his hands down. Then he took a solid kendo swat across the chest. Now, his pride is hurt, and he's quitting — taking the geographic cure by popping back to Georgia. He's going back there with the burden of entitlement and specialness strapped like a monkey on his back.

Georgia is only a "simple place and time" to him because the variables are somewhat more consistent. If he had stayed and accepted the larger order, he might, in fact, have become the star he wanted to be. But to be a star, you have to play in many New Jersey clubs and spend time on the road of life. You have to see the Big Picture — the deeper lesson system. You have to walk up your own mountain and go beyond the *need* for stardom.

There is no such thing as a second self. *We each have only one self, one life.* The man in the song will be the same person whether he's in Georgia or L.A. He's like Brer Rabbit in the classic Disney film "Song of the South." Frustrated with his own "lesson plan," Brer Rabbit decided to run away. He set out from the briar patch despite Brer Bear's wise admonition that "you can't leave your troubles behind."

It wasn't long before Brer Rabbit, loaded with feelings of entitlement, dependency and desire to be appreciated, ran into the Tar Baby. Being a typical Lone Ranger caretaker, Brer Rabbit tried to correct — to change — Tar Baby, who had refused to say hello. You probably know the rest of the story. Brer Rabbit became so angry that he hit Tar Baby and stuck fast to him.

Poor Brer Rabbit. He had left the briar patch because he felt manipulated and controlled. And what happened? He walked right into even more control (literal stuckness), motivated by his drive for acceptance from the outside world.

Wise Brer Bear was the master. But Brer Rabbit wasn't listening. The student wasn't ready. The lesson was there, but he didn't hear it.

You can find other lessons in movies, theater and television. If you're thinking in terms of the larger order, you can even learn from soap operas, which are awash with dependency patterns and confusing boundaries. The draw, the attraction to the viewer, is the idea that lies, manipulation, deceit, gossip and generalized gratification can be learned and do work. If those characters can survive doing such awful things, surely there wouldn't be a painful price for the small things you or I might pull off. Right? Wrong. The soaps regularly demonstrate that dependency *doesn't* work. The lessons are there, but they aren't accepted. It is an illusion to think that if we practice wrong actions, we can get things right.

Music, particularly the blues or country and western, offers many new lesson opportunities if only we would listen to the underlying attachment message. Expectation. Disappointment. Trains, rain, highways, alcohol, sexual affairs, rejected love, prison and victimhood become the audio soap operas of life. One humorous example that comes to mind is the Waylon Jennings song "Take Your Tongue Out Of My Mouth, I'm Kissing You Goodbye."

Denial of change can create considerable pain. Unbalanced relationships offer difficult lessons for adjustment. Almost every song we hear plays on the emotions of that "perfect moment sometime in the past." The words and music form a wailful moan for the safety and protection of the childhood home. The protagonists in these songs often miss their lesson opportunities and choose illusions of safety, of gratification. They carry their memories down that lonely, rainy highway. While their *minds* ride the roads, they leave their *hearts* at the truck stops of life. They want to go back to Georgia. They seek the illusions of a perfect relationship, crying over their pain and hoping the catharsis will make it better. But crying *won't* change your life. Only action will. If you accept the lessons, the whole journey changes.

WORK

Work is an everyday experience — but we don't know how to use it for our own development. Many people aren't connected with what they're doing. They aren't emotionally involved with the activity, the process, of their work effort. They work from the head instead of from the heart *and* mind, because they don't see the connections, the value or the contribution of what they do. Their emotional isolation from their own activities leads to low-quality products and job dissatisfaction. Their work is only a means to an end, and they do their jobs in order to arrive somewhere out in the future. The money they make will, in their minds, provides that future. They live empty days for a remote future time.

So often, we use our minds to disconnect and manipulate rather than to connect and integrate. We've all heard the adage, "If it ain't broke, don't fix it." That remark seems to tell you to drive your car until it does break, and then let the mechanic have it. Run your life out to the stops and then hand it over to your partner (or a shrink) to fix it. If your car is missing one spark plug, it may run for awhile in spite of that problem. But if you don't correct that plug, the car will eventually break down completely. Self-maintenance! Self-maintenance! Small adjustments are necessary to stay on track.

Other people can't fix you, but they can show you how to fix yourself. My own job as a psychiatrist is self-limiting if done right. You may need assistance from someone for the short run, but if you pay attention to your own lessons, you eventually will be on your own. You'll be able to take care of yourself. You'll find your own true nature.

Many years ago, I read *Zen and the Art of Motorcycle Maintenance*, a book that shows how our relationships with even inanimate objects can teach us about our own self-maintenance. The protagonist of this book was spiritually connected to his bike. He understood its language. But he lost contact with himself when he tried to analyze the meaning of quality. He became caught up in the polemics between objective and subjective thought. The book's interesting closing reveals how disconnected he had been from his son, while he was clearly so connected with the workings of the machine. He could fix his bike, but not his relationships. He was out of balance, despite having a deep awareness of the lessons learned from the machine. Ultimately, he was able to transpose the lessons to the relationship with his son.

One swallow doesn't make a summer. Human relationships are more complex than a relationship with a motorcycle. But *any* animate or inanimate relationship can teach us about ourselves, *if* we seek the larger understanding. If we can apply the lessons across the board rather than only in focused areas of attention, we'll find ourselves more in balance.

Many people can apply the principles of Big Picture thinking to others. Or, perhaps they can apply it to certain aspects of their own lives — their jobs, their motorcycles, their hobbies. But Big Picture awareness is hardest to apply to the relationships we care most about. The more intimate we become, the more variables and boundaries we must recognize and accept.

So often, our lives are spot-welded by aggregate pockets of understanding in a variety of different places. And yet, you don't have to be a metallurgist to know that spot welds are weaker than a good continuous weld. It's like three blind men describing an elephant. The unfolding of your life story depends on which aspects you choose to emphasize and which you "forget" to see.

Through larger order thinking, we can discover the amalgam of connections available in our most loving and difficult relationships. In nature, in the larger order, every relationship counts. Every relationship can offer important lessons. The connections in our most important relationships offer us special opportunities for self-discovery and personal evolution. Through our growing awareness of these connections, we can begin to appreciate how the balance process takes place.

RELATIONSHIP BALANCE

In our close and special relationships, we often find our feelings out of balance. We must seek balance through connection, without attachment, to all things — relationships, jobs, the environment. Our ecology *is* us. *Our relationships mirror the level at which our own self-esteem functions.* If we're over-connected and attached, we lose focus. If we're under-connected, life is boring and meaningless. Bored kids don't see the connections; neither do bored adults.

If we can truly see our relationships, we can see ourselves. We select partners at work or home that are manifestations of our own self-esteem. Our partner problems and partner choices are manifestations of our internal conflicts and personal blinders. The characteristics of those relationships — both where they are balanced, and where they swing out of balance — can teach us about our own limitations. At no time is this more evident than when one partner in a relationship decides to become more self-reflective and to seek the higher order. Such self-reflection — through therapy, reading, or self-help groups — can cause the relationship to be thrown out of balance. The other partner, who is not growing within the context of the relationship, exerts a pull that comes from the fear of abandonment — the fear of being alone. That pull, which can be exceedingly strong, can either drive the growing partner away or pull him back to stasis.

This kind of dependency pattern is often seen near the end of adolescence when the family seeks to maintain control. Increased control in later adolescence can inevitably drive the child away for years. Similar patterns of fear and control can drive spouses away as each partner struggles to set the agenda for the other, motivated by jealousy, insecurity, comparisons, etc. The dependency-oriented spot welds of insecurity all become evident over time. As years pass and the relationship changes, the spot welds are either eliminated through the development of a larger relationship, or they grow more weak and uncertain with each new reality experience inside or outside of the relationship.

With each new responsibility, the relationship can suffer new stresses that confront old dependency patterns. If he gets a promotion, she may become anxious and unbalanced. If she experiences trauma or difficulty, the patterns are challenged for both. As partners resolve these dependency patterns and control issues, trust develops. Non-resolution, or silence and painful resentment, brings more distrust. We must actively encourage the development of our partners while, at the same time, seek our own personal development. This encouragement should take place in every relationship reality — at home, at work, with the kids, etc. Mutual development brings balance. Attachments to old patterns bring elements of avoidance and control.

BALANCE AND FEELINGS

A simple feeling chart can encourage a better understanding of the way difficult feelings can be turned into learning opportunities. In various psychiatric hospitals, I've seen the formation of groups to deal with specific feelings: anger groups, depression groups, etc. The mission of these groups is confusing, but it seems to be predicated upon the idea that placement in such a group will "get the feelings out." Participants quickly become bored once they've demonstrated those feelings. Their next question is, "What do we do after that?" The question regularly presents itself: How can feelings be (usefully) integrated into the self-development process?

The following diagram has proven helpful as it gives Lone Rangers and Helpless Victims *specific feeling goals* for the recovery process.

WISDOM

SERENITY   **COURAGE**

RESPECTFUL SELF-PROTECTION

LONE RANGER
Affect: **mad**
Attitude: **pride**
Disrespect of others
Excessive respect of
self

BALANCE

HELPLESS VICTIM
Affect: **sad**
Attitude: **self pity**
Excessive respect of
others
Disrespect of self

Let go of control; acceptance of others

Let go of avoidance; acceptance of self

BALANCE

ACTION

Killing
Hitting others
Gestures, throwing things

Suicide
Hitting or hurting self

VERBAL

Shouting
Angry words
Sarcasm
Harumphing

Crying/sobbing
Shouting
Gossip
Whining

BALANCE

OUT OF BALANCE

OUT OF BALANCE

NON-VERBAL

Angry looks
Impatient signs
Eye rolling
Squirming/tapping

Sad looks
Sighs of hurt
Eyes downcast
Withdrawal

OUT OF BALANCE

OUT OF BALANCE

FEAR

REALITY
Change proceeds at its own pace.
Patterns in others either **change** or **remain the same.**

The fear of ever-changing relationship reality creates a discomfort that shifts the attention between self and others. The scale shows how some people can escalate from a state of slight non-verbal discomfort to being completely out of control. It's common to see people shift from one method of coping to another: from sadness to anger, or from non-verbal to verbal or even to action, as their pressure builds. Ultimately, in a worst-case scenario, they may kill themselves, someone else or both. The fundamental reason why people go berserk is that they can't take the reality as it is at that moment. They become increasingly victimized by their own failure to manage the reality, or by others who encourage their entitlement to destructive action. At the worst moments, they flip back and forth between control and avoidance. But, manipulation, anger, lies, pleading or tears won't change the facts. Your feelings don't change reality. All we can change is our own attitude about reality and change.

In recovery, your feelings are your guide back to the reality you can't accept. They are your opportunity to discover your attachments — your patterns. If you are out of balance, your feelings are your responsibility. Use your anger and sadness to discover your own expectations.

CONTROL IS AVOIDANCE AND AVOIDANCE IS CONTROL

The small things that we do in a relationship can teach us about balance. Nostalgia is a teddy bear; the future is a dream. Insightful, connected *action* must take place in the moment. Connection is neither too controlled nor too avoidant. We must train our eyes to see with deeper vision and to search for the deeper knowledge that exists in small behaviors.

Deep knowledge is to be aware of disturbance before disturbance, to be aware of danger before danger, to be aware of destruction before destruction, to be aware of calamity before calamity. Strong action is training the body without being burdened by the body, exercising the mind without being used by the mind, working in the world without being affected by the world, carrying out tasks without being obstructed by tasks.

By deep knowledge of principle, one can change disturbance into order, change danger into safety, change destruction into survival, change calamity into fortune. By strong action on the way, one can bring the body to the realm of longevity, bring the mind to the sphere of mystery, bring the world to great peace, and bring tasks to great fulfillment.

> *Sun Tzu, Chinese Warrior-*
> *Philosopher*

Deep knowledge can come from great pain or from small, apparently insignificant activities. From the book *Chop Wood and Carry Water* comes another important insight: "Marvelous power, marvelous action! Chopping wood, carrying water."

Chopping wood for the purpose of being warmed by a fire sometime in the future can make the chopping a drudgery. Chopping wood to experience the outdoors — the sound of the ax, the split and smell of the wood, the sweat and the cool wind — can be a purpose in itself. It can connect you with the Balance Order. It is what your mind decides your purpose is. If you seek only comfort and gratification, you'll long for the warm fire and angrily force yourself to chop wood. You will avoid the moment. If you are in the lesson process and are already a student, you may learn more about yourself with an ax and a pile of wood than you bargained for.

Many men go fishing their entire lives without knowing that it is not fish they are after.

> *Henry David Thoreau*
> *American Writer*

If you can't immediately connect with your relationships and activities, set appropriate short-term goals. Make plans to change your viewpoint. Seek the connection in everything that you're doing in order to find your real self. The impediments of work are lesson opportunities for the willing student. But work and motorcycles are only one aspect of the big picture.

COMFORT ZONE

So many people today are talking about the comfort zone. Now, at this point in the book, we can understand it better. The comfort zone is your personal comfort space with upper *and* lower limits. We can become uncomfortable doing well or doing poorly. The comfort zone parameters exist wherever change takes place. If we were to lose money, that would obviously take us out of our comfort zone on the lower end, because money can buy temporary comfort and distractions. Those of you who are working on yourself already know of the comfort zone problem on the upper end — the difficult edge of more success.

Freud himself wrote a paper many years ago called "Those Wrecked By Success." Such people are unable to handle the additional feelings of responsibility that come with success. Yet anyone, as Sun Tzu pointed out over 2,000 years ago, who follows the deep knowledge principle can bring the world to great peace. Individuals who follow the precepts and practice the deep recovery process outlined in these pages, will attract more responsibility. It's like that Theory of Circumvential Direction. If you *chase* responsibility, it eludes you. If you *live* responsibility, it comes to you automatically. If you search for a relationship, you can't find one. If you let go of searching and form a relationship with yourself, people immediately appear. Through respectful self-protection in relationships, you will find balance.

Many are shocked by the speed with which new responsibility comes their way. The change is a surprise. It's unexpected.

> *Unless you expect the unexpected you will never find (truth) for it's hard to discover and hard to attain.*
> *Heraclitus, 500 B.C.*

Prepare now for the unexpected new responsibilities that will come your way. Know that a consistent demonstration of competence and strong action at your current level of functioning will bring a quick response and new responsibilities.

Either advances or retreats in your life circumstance can bring problems if you aren't aware of the oscillation process. The Midnight Train is an opportunity for self-discovery. It's a moment of reflection between life events. It's on the down side of your comfort zone. It is a time to catch your breath, so you won't have expectations. You can now expect the unexpected, and the unexpected will be your teacher.

A heroin addict I know had four years of chemical recovery (straight time) and four years of recovery work on his personal self-development program. Like Gandhi, he was bringing himself along. He got a new job; a new house; a fine, new car and had recently remarried. And what do you think happened? He started using heroin again. He still *thought* of himself as a heroin addict, even though he was straight. He topped out of his comfort zone. He did not have a warrior's mind and was not prepared for the unexpected. Fearful of success, he was a street person who was afraid to leave the street for a different reality.

One definition of "crazy" is: *repeating the same actions, but expecting different results.* This book is designed to help make you uncrazy — to change your actions. But, if you *do* something different — if you take a different action — be ready for different results. Be ready for both the benefits and the setbacks.

SPORTS AND PLAY

We've seen deep recovery principles reflected in music, work and ancient aphorisms. Let's look at two other everyday experiences — sports and play. Attachment and avoidance are so often connected. They are like winning and losing. Why are some people obsessed with sports? Often it's because they're focused solely on winning. The only thing that matters to them is who won and lost. From the World Series to the Super Bowl, the question is always, "Who's on top?" As Vince Lombardi once said: "Winning isn't everything, but wanting to win is." My point is that wanting to win can also kill you. Life is not in the winning. It's in the game itself. Remember the expression we mentioned earlier, "He who dies with the most toys wins." It's not true. Winning is an illusion — those who win know that. The real game is with yourself and how you're handling your own reality. The real game is not quitting. It is walking firmly and courageously down the path of our own personal reality, striving for our personal best. We must always watch our desire to find the end points, the arrivals and the titles. Each can bring the illusion of temporary power. Many such "winners" are really losers. Winning isn't everything. Wanting to do your personal best in life is.

My father asked me to memorize a single short verse during my childhood. It was on a old tin plaque, a promotional item from a hardware store.

For when the one Great Scorer comes
To write against your name,
He marks — not that you won or lost—
But how you played the game.
Grantland Rice

The "how" is the process, the evolution over time. Seeking our true nature is an ongoing process and has nothing to do with the illusions of arrivals and perfection. It is not limited by the concept of time. It laughs at the drive to end the season — to lock down this moment as the best. Best effort is not best score. It's how you play the game. It's how you are today against how you were yesterday. It's how you handle winning and how you handle losing. If we change *how* we live, we value best effort and honest play. We are courageous in victory or defeat.

Others may react uncomfortably to our courage. They fear for our safety and say we are foolish. They tell us what our other friends are saying about our attitude and our slight movement away from gossip, negativism and comparisons. Why do they do this? Because if we change, they must begin to reflect on *their own* way of dealing with reality. It suggests change for them as well. They are pushed into deeper self-reflection. They, too, must cast off illusions and must begin to address attachments and dependencies. They must let go of control. If they don't, we will have more problems with them as they try to pull us into their frightened, limited perceptual system.

THE RAPIDS PROCESS: GETTING UNSTUCK IN RECOVERY

Now, you're set for the adventure of your life. There is a Huck Finn opportunity in the days ahead. As you travel down the river of life, as you seek your own true nature, you'll find a Deep Recovery order to self-discovery that works the same way for everyone. The order is simple and consistent. As you float the sometimes quiet river, remain prepared. Don't be surprised by the reality of the rapids. The word *RAPIDS* is an acronym for the process of self-development. The river *RAPIDS* are the inevitable, rapidly changing realities that you will face. They will teach you. This is how the lesson process evolves — how it awakens you from your superficial dreams of consistency.

R = R E A L I T Y

In the first part of your journey, you float along through life, dreaming lazily with few variables other than the sun, the sky and the gentle tug of the current. You are, for a while, protected by your family and comforted with the illusion of control. But over time, you become aware of the *Reality* of forthcoming changes. You hear the roar of real rapids in the distance. It's the sound of unmovable rocks and repetitive relationship problems. Your relationships are your real challenges. Some you can handle easily; others present real impediments. You discover that you can't change others. Their position is fixed. The rapids of the past haunt you. These fixed impediments are worrisome because they remind you that *you* must make adjustments — that you must change your own perceptions, that you must change yourself.

A = ATTACHMENTS

With any new (or old) fixed reality, you can become frightened. You feel alone on your journey. Fear of dealing with that changing reality encourages you to seek *attachments* — old gratifications, old relationship patterns and other distractions that bring illusions of safety. You long for *permanent* connections to people, places, and things such as sex, alcohol, drugs and relationships. You seek to fix yourself in time and to stop the change. You may search for an altered state of consciousness. You seek to be one traveller and travel both paths. You become a victim of your attachments, your old relationship patterns. You seek safety in LR and HV patterns and in the nostalgia of the past. You save your amulets, diplomas and your teddy bears. Fear of the rapids causes you to grab at branches that hang from the banks. You want to stop the change. You want to "go back to Georgia." Your thoughts are reductionistic and categorical — from all bad to all good. Attachments are a temporary Band-Aid on your brain and on your pain. Attachments can be something as simple as shopping or as complex as complete relationship relapse. They can easily become naturally repetitive and beyond your control. They often become automatic, beyond awareness. They can be unconscious or conscious. And, they inevitably create a victim role.

P = PAIN

Your old safety attachment patterns create your victim *pain*. The branches tear at your hands, as the current of life pulls you along. By hanging on, you create your own problems. Attachment pain begins when we're young and continues all the way through life. When you're down and out, you cry for your teddy bears. Your teddy bears can be your home, your car, your corner office, your title or a sexual affair — anything that temporarily comforts you. But, those things can also cause pain if you hang onto them too long, or if you use them to define yourself. You will be hurt by your self-created victim roles — through unbalanced LR or HV relationship patterns, through dependencies and through addictions. These attachments, like the branch, bring pain. The natural order of change and time cannot be stopped. The river flows on. Others may remain fixed or change at different rates. We create more pain when, out of balance, we try to avoid or control our personal reality. Pain is the price we pay for avoiding or controlling reality through attachments.

I = INSIGHT

Your pain can teach you. When the student is ready, the lesson appears. Pain gives you the opportunity for *insight* and the chance to see, from the higher ground, the Big Picture sacred mountain. It can encourage deep recovery. Through your pain, you can achieve comprehension of how the whole operation works. There is little true insight without pain. Insight shows you that you can change only some things — your own perspective, your own behavior. Without insight, you recycle through the attachments and pain. Through insight, you can see *your own hand* hanging on to the branch. Your life is your own responsibility. Most of us recycle until the insight brings an associated new responsibility for self. Insight frees you from being bound in limited awareness, bound in time. But, insight can itself become a malignant attachment as we seek other explanations and slip into the illusion that thinking and pattern recognition are themselves solutions. Intellectual fascism results. True wisdom is knowing what you can and cannot change.

D = DETACH

Insight into attachment pain teaches you that you must *detach*. Release the painful branch. The pain from old attachment patterns teaches you about the river and the journey. It teaches you to let go of control and to get on with facing your own personal reality. It teaches you that prolonged avoidance brings greater pain. If you can detach, you can be more objective about where to go and what to do. Detachment brings the wisdom to know the difference between what we can and cannot change. It brings serenity and acceptance of the larger order. Detachment connects us to the higher order. Along with the insight that you are causing your own pain, comes the

energy to let go of the branch and detach. You discover
that it is actually more painful to hang on than to let go.

S = SPECIFIC ACTION
Our lives will remain in our heads if we don't take *spe-cific action*. Thinking activity is not living activity. Corrective action, balanced and specific, can itself bring fur-
ther understanding. You learn as you directly face your
relationship realities. Enlightened, purposeful action
brings growth. Action can be in the form of silence or waiting. But it is always balanced, decisive and serious. In relationships, you work to practice *respectful self-protection*.
Enlightened action is objective and free of emotional over-
lay. The rocks and currents *require* specific action.
Avoidance is never sufficient. Managing the small rapids
brings skill at larger rapids. Specific actions recycle you directly into and through reality. Your actions must be di-
rected toward running your own perceived rapids. They
must take you back into your own reality — your own true
nature.

*When in doubt, straighten out, that's the boats-
man's motto. Never broach on a rock. Always
face the danger.*

Edward Abbey, Naturalist

RECYCLING

As you progress, you will soon discover that the recovery
process has its own built-in traps. Each new level of the
RAPIDS awareness, each new step in the process, presents an opportunity for apparent safety. Each aspect of
the RAPIDS process can feed your dream state, your illusion system. Each step can lead you to repeat and recycle
through the same familiar territory.
Those who get stuck and cycle only through *Reality* are
Lone Rangers. They rarely accept the pain or vulnerability of the experience of fear. They are reality junkies and
thrill seekers, set on managing the outside world, stuck in
the illusion of the mastery of things.

DEEP RECOVERY / 155

Those repetitively cycling through *Attachments* are many: addicts, alcoholics, Lone Rangers, Helpless Victims, phobics or anyone with dependency issues of any kind. We all have attachment problems at one time or another. We all pattern our responses to the changing world and become frozen in the pattern.

The *Pain* recyclers are obvious: Helpless Victims. They cycle in pain and thereby avoid insight. Their pain keeps them isolated and alone. They grieve for their own self-limited, isolated experience. They recycle as victims back through the same destructive realities.

Insight recyclers are the experts, the nihilists, the recovery junkies, the fundamentalists, the gurus and the cultists. They proclaim that either their way is the *only* way to transform your life, or that there is *no way* to accomplish that transformation (that transformation is itself a lie). They are frozen by thinking and negative judgment, caught up in figuring it out for themselves and others. They know it all, but do nothing.

Some evolved people who see the Big Picture simply *Detach* completely. They work through attachments, pain and insight but get stuck as they detach. They don't talk, work or play. They meditate, pray and leave the patterns of everyday life. They create a separate safe, undisturbed reality that precludes involvement with such tasks as taking out the trash or doing the dishes. Their relationships are minimal or fixed. Mystics, monks and some middle management administrators fit in this niche.

It's important to understand that *a whole lifetime can be lost on any of these cycles.* Each step may look like a step in the right direction, and it is. *But the circle is incomplete without specific action.* A person regularly seeking daily enlightenment may, through *specific action,* flip through the whole RAPIDS process in seconds with each new reality. As some evolve in their understanding, they can go from crying for years, to weeks, to hours, to only a transient feeling of sadness.

The most important cycle is direct, specific, intentional action into and through relationship reality. The action may involve silence or words, action or non-action. It is

balanced and characterized by *respectful self-protection.*
Specific action crashes through the myth of being alone
and disconnected. It seeks compromise and understanding of the larger order. Your conflicts are mirrored by
those in your company. Each specific action presents new
opportunities for further awareness and additional
lessons. The acceptance of each new responsibility brings
additional lesson opportunities. These new responsibilities create possibilities for leadership.

The lessons of that Midnight Train we all ride are
learned through an acceptance of the natural RAPIDS
order. Our realities, our attachments, our relationship
stuckness are all opportunities knocking. As time passes,
changes inevitably occur. Yet, we find ourselves locked in
again and again by our paleolithic tapes and our relationship attachment patterns. We overlook the flow of our
stream. We look to the banks for rescue and hope that if
we cry out, things will change. We mistake rage for
courage and search for the safety of old patterns — of
home.

But there is no home out there. There are no enemies,
either. There is only your growing awareness of the lesson
process. The closest you can get to finding home is to
search within. Your home exists in the consistent *process*
of knowing your self.

9

Recovery In Action:

Cold Calling Enlightenment

Know the enemy and know yourself; in a hundred battles you will never be in peril. When you're ignorant of the enemy but know yourself, your chances of winning or losing are equal. If ignorant of the enemy and yourself you are certain in every battle to be in peril.

Sun Tzu
Chinese Warrior-Philosopher

YOU CANNOT LEARN ABOUT OTHERS BY STAYING AT HOME within yourself. John LeCarre said it in *The Looking Glass War:* "There was an immeasurable gulf between those who went and those who stayed behind." Each new reality in our lives brings both risk *and* opportunity. The reality of Vietnam created an immeasurable gulf in our nation. It was a gulf of misunderstanding, of disconnection. But Vietnam was also a painful lesson. It was a lesson in what we as a nation could and could not do. We did not know the enemy. We did not know ourselves. It was a painful lesson in national self-awareness. Out of that lesson came the opportunity to think more carefully about our global goals, our national efforts and our caretaking attitude. Vietnam taught us to take a deeper look at ourselves.

Each new task or relationship can bring new learning opportunities or more problems depending on your perspective. In this process of self-discovery, one can travel the world or never leave Dubuque, Iowa. A change in geography isn't as important as a change in attitude about whatever reality your geography offers. Your personal reality can teach you about yourself.

I once had an occasion, in a rush of apparent sophistication, to observe to one of my Philadelphia analytic mentors that "the Midwest is so provincial." She quickly countered, "Dr. Parker, there's nowhere quite as provincial as Philadelphia."

At the psychoanalytic meetings in New York that same year, I had an interesting conversation in the Waldorf Astoria with a fellow trainee. We established that she was from Manhattan, whereupon she asked about my home. "Philadelphia," I replied rather proudly. "Oh" she said, and murmured, "I see," as she turned away. Manhattan itself can be provincial. It depends upon your attitude.

Cold calling is a marketing term which describes the process of developing new sales opportunities from a previously unknown population. Door-to-door sales is a form of cold calling. Each new person, each new door, becomes an opportunity without the security of knowing something about the response beforehand. Cold calling is a process that bridges the gulf of misunderstanding that occurs between people. Through cold calling, you interface more with others and open to the larger order. Cold calling is far more than a marketing technique — it is a way of opening yourself up to information from others. It is a connecting exchange of information. It is not a change in location; it is a change in perception. It is a learning attitude. It is wisdom in specific action. Cold calling is your private ticket to the universal order.

TEDDY BEARS

In the development of children and adults, there are phases of growth characterized by separation and individuation. This process unfolds as each individual grows more able to function autonomously. In childhood, one of the characteristic manifestations of the separation and individuation process is the Teddy Bear. It's warm and fuzzy and anthropomorphic — an imaginary, nurturing "mother" you can hold close in bed to forestall the worries of the night. It is a normal developmental stage that temporarily solves the problem of feeling alone. Child psychiatrists call the Teddy Bear a "transitional object." It offers transitional support in the developmental space between being with mother and being alone. It's like the memories of childhood on that Midnight Train to Georgia. Transitional objects have existed since the days of the caveman in the form of mother goddess figures, amulets, magical tokens, etc. Today, they take many forms such as children's blankets, lucky charms, memorabilia, nostalgic songs, photographs, words and concepts. Your provincial Teddy Bear could even be New York City. If you're overpowered by your Teddy Bear, you're stuck. There is an immeasurable gulf between those who are open to new experience and those who are closed.

THE GROUP TEDDY BEAR

When people gather together to handle a common difficult reality, they form tribes, bands, clubs, nations and businesses that are characterized by mutual efforts towards achieving a common goal. These groups can also take on transitional meanings of security. The memorabilia of life recall those moments of shared apprehension. The school rings, college decals, company shirts and club lapel pins all tell others who your tribal members are and what difficult reality trials you have mastered. There is an element of safety and comfort in the nurture of the group. The group is supportive, but if it's a strong developmental one, it encourages your personal development — just as a healthy mother would encourage her child to take on increasing degrees of self-responsibility. An unhealthy group, on the other hand, helps keep you closed to others.

There are also less formal groups characterized by certain dress and behavior codes of the individuals who band together to handle different segments of reality. Often they can be seen waving at each other even though they've never met: motorcyclists, long-haul truckers, boaters, sailors, hunters, surfers, etc.

When I was a kid, there were two groups: the "hoods" and the rest of us. Now, our adolescent population is overwhelmed with many subgroups: heads, grits, preps, punkers, posers (pose as punkers), rappers, jocks, socialites, skaters, surfers, brains, rednecks, satanists, witches, beboppers, gangs, etc. They each have certain language, dress and behavior patterns. The group members are mutually attracted and use the group as a home base against the rapidly changing outside world. The group is their Teddy Bear of mutual support.

These Teddy Bear pieces of our past can all keep us from becoming ourselves if we become or remain attached. Each attachment is a potentially seductive home that can ultimately become a trap. The Teddy Bear is a potential trap, because it is an illusion of safety. I've seen it happen in all kinds of groups, even those that are supposed to encourage personal development.

Religious groups, for example, which, on the one hand, encourage humility, can be paradoxically unbalanced as they encourage Lone Ranger entitlement patterns: "We're the best." "We're special; we're entitled." "Anybody who doesn't see it the way we do will not be saved." But didn't Christ say, "Let he who is without sin cast the first stone"? The problem with entitlement is that it makes you feel frustrated with, and superior to, the rest of the world. Some recovery groups can discourage development by sending out the message that "you don't need others, you only need us." Any group, even those seeking balance, can become unbalanced and overprotective.

Balanced recovery groups aren't as concerned with how bad your life has been, as with what you're *doing* about it. Recovery groups can be *unbalanced* in either one of two ways. They can be Lone Ranger, hard-core "expert groups" who "know" recovery, or they can be victim groups that share pain.

The unbalanced Lone Ranger "support" groups are frequently angry, negative, judgmental and controlling. Their action as a group is to berate and "break the denial." New members who can put up with their tyranny are obviously as hard core as the rest. They wear their sickness like merit badges. They are proud that they are no longer vulnerable. They are experts at the recovery process, but they can't handle personal relationships. "I almost died three times." "I lost everything." "I was so sick, I even used while I was flying cross country." These are typical remarks for these groups. They feel that anger, resentment, control, goading, and unbalanced confrontation will lead new members to honesty. It's a hazing initiation. Their recovery experience makes them experts and gives them the right to be disrespectful. These groups become important through the denial present in others — they feel they are perfect, they're well, they're free of denial.

The Helpless Victim groups are there to dump affect. They are hurt by others. Theirs isn't a war of expertise, but one of pain, unhappiness, futility and mistakes. Their competition is not one of purple hearts and near-death experience, but one of victimhood and negativity about others and how they've been mistreated by a world that doesn't understand.

The Lone Ranger group tries to recover through learning how to be strong with growling criticism. Helpless Victims hope to be cured through emotional release and hugs. Lone Rangers say, "I've recovered, I'm back again. I can take anything." Helpless Victims say, "I'll never be able to take it. Please support my deficiencies. Love me in spite of my defective self." Both groups offer an illusion of comfort, a Teddy Bear of protection. They offer a pattern fit.

In chemical dependency recovery groups, there are really two recoveries: one from chemicals and one from emotional dependency/counterdependency. The "drunkalog" is a Helpless Victim statement. It is a long whine. A *complaint is not recovery planning or action.* Dumping creates victimhood for both the Dumper and the Dumpee. People can work on recovery from chemical dependency but overlook recovery from their psychological dependency patterns. Anyone can remain out of balance in an out-of-balance group.

The long complaints in some support meetings about "what *somebody* did," are victim statements also. The issue should be: What do *you* do? How can *you* become responsible without feeling guilty? How do *you* break your own cycle of repetition? The answer is very simple: Take consistent, direct, recovery action. Set limits. Exercise regularly. Practice self-care. Take ownership of your life. If your recovery group is a victim group that encourages dependency patterns, it becomes your new responsibility to encourage a change in the group focus. If you doubt these observations, just attend a few speakers' meetings. Victim meetings leave you feeling sick. Positive action speakers, who show how they succeeded, light the way. Groups don't like either LR or HV patterns; they appreciate self-responsibility.

On the other hand, if your group encourages the feeling that you're special and better than others, that x number of years in recovery makes you an expert, or that the rest of the world is screwed up, then you're in a sick group. Such a group takes a categorical, fixed position of good and bad, black and white. Such charisma seekers long for pat, categorical answers that separate people and offer illusions of protection. The gangs in Los Angeles are killing each other over categorically sick positions scrawled symbolically on the sides of buildings.

We now can understand that the next specific recovery step is different for each personal circumstance. The victim pain is the same for everyone. The caretaker guilt is the same. But groups differ. If the group regularly motivates its members toward advancing degrees of personal responsibility and cold-calling connections in daily living, as do most spiritual/mental health and recovery groups, then there is no problem. But if the group sets itself up as the provider of awareness and enlightenment, then it's encouraging a dependency position. *Remember: The lessons come from your own awareness of your own pain, and the resolution of your own guilt.* Growth comes from fully accepting your own lessons and taking corrective action with your own personal experience of reality.

I used to work with a woman who was intelligent and strikingly attractive. In addition to talking about dependency issues with me, she had participated for years in a nationally prominent psycho-educational group with a charismatic leader. He set himself up as a "expert" in self-realization. Ultimately, the woman and he had an affair, and he quickly rejected her. As a child, she had been molested by her father. When, in tears, she courageously confronted the leader about his betrayal of trust, he interpreted it all as her problem. "You shouldn't have thought of me as your father," was his response. He blamed her, even though *he* was supposed to be the teacher. She had been chasing the charisma, the illusory safety and special comfort of his power and his group. But no group, no person, can take care of you. No one has the right to blame you for their shortcomings. Idealizing a group or a person will lead to disappointment.

A balanced group can, on the other hand, urge you on. It will teach cold calling. Most of us feel so entitled and special that we only want private consultants. We want to be handled privately, personally and specially. We want to think alone. We want to solve it ourselves. There is, of course, a place for private matters, but healthy healing *groups* are developmentally beneficial. They can be intimidating. But, working in the context of a group is part of bringing yourself along. It can be an exercise group, a recovery group or even a book club. Groups cut through the entitlement. At the local Wareing's Gym, the Wareing brothers and the A.M. crew expect you to be there and accept no excuses. Theirs is a good natured balance of structure and encouragement. Working *with* a group without being worked *by* it is an important cold calling step.

Cold calling, the process of knocking on new doors, is a necessary and fundamental part of self-discovery. It is an action that must be undertaken daily, because it breaks your illusory safety patterns. Learn to be critical of your own tendency to remain in the comfort of home or the comfort of your own group. Seek beyond the dumping process, beyond the blame. Balanced development is looking for the lessons, rather than just waiting for lessons to happen to you. You can't bring your tennis game along by becoming the best in your group but never playing with new partners. If you think of life as a retail store, you'll only be able to interact with those who come in the door ready to buy. Life can easily become a passive process in which you feel you must wait for your enlightenment. It is, therefore, important to set specific goals for the recovery process. Cold calling can take you out of the store.

YOUR GARDEN

People seeking self-discovery frequently talk about boundaries. Before the Big Picture starts to dawn on us, we may be either a serious Lone Ranger with excessive boundaries or a confused Helpless Victim who can hardly set any boundaries at all.

You know your lesson plan involves taking action like cold calling, but where and how? Through the process of changing the repetitive patterns of everyday life comes the increasing awareness that you *do* have to stick up for yourself or you *will be victimized*. But what do you stick up for?

Imagine, from now on, that you have a garden — the garden of your own self. Your garden is your self-development, self-discovery practice. It includes your developing sense of personal values. However, if you're like most people, your name isn't even in your own daily appointment book. You must start by regularly placing your own name into your own appointment book. Otherwise, you run on everybody else's agenda. Your garden will not only go to weeds, but it will turn into a playground for others.

Your garden must have a fence. Otherwise, your friends, your spouse or your children will step on your squash and rutabagas. They'll walk all over everything you've planted and then say, "Oh, I'm sorry. I didn't know you had your own garden." Setting your own schedule and taking some time for yourself is not a matter of "entitlement," "rights," or "selfishness." It is simple self-protection and sustenance, much like combing your hair or taking a bath. If you don't systematically address goals you have set for yourself, you'll be enslaved by your own drive to care for everyone else. To neglect to set up your own fence or to schedule your own self-awareness track is an obvious setup for victimhood. It means you aren't paying attention.

If, conversely, your granite fences are too high and guarded by cannons, if your garden is perfect and you haven't seen a neighbor in weeks (because they're afraid you'll shoot them), then you're a gardening addict — a Lone Ranger safety addict. You're stuck on the concept of self-protection and you can't shoot the breeze or connect. You measure your radishes with a micrometer.

Fence maintenance and repair must be regularly practiced in a respectful manner. The fence is your opportunity to practice balance, to appropriately connect or detach. There are four magic words to use when somebody tries to jump over your fence: *"I have a problem..."* Just fill in the blanks with what the problem is.

If someone is standing on your squash, stay calm. The person may not know it. He may be on autopilot like that old farmer's mule we talked about earlier. He doesn't even know he's hit the tree. So, pull out your four magic words and say them with gravity the *moment* you perceive the intrusion, or else your garden will be ruined. Make the remarks personal and private. This is not a group matter. Take the person off into another room. Take a tip from the Navy Bluejacket Manual: "Private criticism, public praise." Don't whine or fuss about how you feel, because it's a waste of time. The person won't care. How *you* feel is *your* business, and if you tell them, you become a victim. "I have a problem ... you're standing on my squash." That's enough. He'll probably say, "Oh, I didn't know." Or, he may bait you and attempt to start an argument by saying, "You're angry with me." But, your anger is for *you* to handle, not for others.

To dump your anger on the other person is a guilt-provoking manipulation born of your own dependency needs. If you do happen to become angry, save discussion until your anger is under control. Business is business. Handle your garden like a business, and have respect for the other person even if he or she is disrespectful of you. Now, if you have respectfully told them several times to get out, but they persist, then you have to ask yourself why you planted a garden near theirs in the first place. You're the victim if you continue to give them the opportunity to walk on your rutabagas. And that includes family members, who have no special privilege with your garden. What you decide to share with anyone is your own choice.

THE UNENLIGHTENED

As you read on, you are becoming a "sentient" being. You're developing an awareness about the deep knowledge of natural world order. You're more aware of your own desire to manipulate and control and your own wish for the Teddy Bear safety of illusions and gratification. You're also aware of your struggle with fear and your desire to avoid change. As you go cold calling, you will quickly see there are many who have not begun to think this deeply about the passing scene. In fact, they don't care about the Big Picture one bit. They haven't had enough pain yet. They haven't found themselves down on the mat looking up at the bright lights. They are still dancing away in avoidance. They are there to test your progress.

As you grow in awareness, you will find yourself attracted to people who themselves are seeking deep knowledge, and you will quickly see pressures mounting from those in denial who are not. The frightened denial group pulls you to join their huddle. Denial and gratification are based on fear. As you become less frightened, more balanced and less a victim, you may become subtly intimidating to those who aren't so self-reflective. They may perceive you as a threat, even though you haven't been disrespectful. They are fearful that you might reject them. You become frightening as you seek to detach from petty dependencies and to join larger world order in acceptance of change.

Those who aren't in the recovery process are either disrespectful and controlling or permissive and non-assertive. They are out of balance. They try to provoke guilt. The people who suffer from attachments and fear are frightened of non-attachment. They need and want you, but they are unable to engage you in primitive games. They see you as selfish, because they can't make you feel guilty. Anger can't be used against you, because you're fearless. You remain calm. They are uncomfortable under these circumstances and will try to get involved in "your problem." But you're already handling your problem. You don't need them to handle you, but they feel they still need *you* to handle *their* problems. They are coming close to a grand illumination. They are about to be disappointed by their expectations. Their Helpless Victim position will only encourage rejection by others.

There are still others who aren't *overtly* dependent and guilt-provoking. They can hurt you through the illusions of protection that they offer and withhold. They tempt you with promises of your success. They look as though they're successful in life, because they have power or money. They frequently remind you what they've done for you. They are experts at *subtle* guilt provocation and blame. Often they will be angry when you are too "foolish" and "frightened" to be with them. Their insecurity becomes quickly apparent when you don't play their game. They are perfect and you are imperfect. They remind you that you are dispensable and that you make mistakes.

There are several important guidelines for handling the people who don't understand the changes in your behavior:

1. RESPECT: Always strive to be respectful of their blindness. It wasn't long ago that you were as blind as they. Remember the pain of your own disappointment when you learned you had to do it yourself. Remembering your own pain will help you remain calm with their pleading and manipulation. Do *with* them, not *for* them. There is no reason to be angry at them or sad for them. There is no reason to be angry at their disrespect, because they don't understand the Big Picture. Caretaking is disrespectful.

2. DETACHMENT: They will be clinging and pulling for an attachment with you. If you caretake them and shield them from reality, you only postpone their lessons. You encourage them to be dependent on you, perpetuating their cycles of pain. There is always a price paid for caretaking others or for seeking to be taken care of.

3. FORGIVENESS: Those who have hurt you did so for various reasons. If they were disrespectful, dishonest and manipulative with you, remember that you per-

mitted it by remaining there. You hadn't learned the lesson yet. You must choose to take either something positive or something negative out of the events that have happened to you at the hands of other people. All events have many negative and positive possibilities. If you focus on the negative, you will continue to blame the other person for the rest of your life. Accepting the positive lesson will free you from the attachment to the pain. The person who hurt you, and the illusion of safety you had prior to being hurt, were lesson opportunities. If they hit you when your hands were down, you could say that they were taking advantage. Conversely, you might choose to recognize that theirs was an important lesson. They taught you to be prepared and more observant next time. If someone consciously and openly tries to give you a lesson, it is for you to develop appreciation for their effort (even if they didn't give the lesson correctly). Succinctly stated, use the pain for enlightenment and insight, regardless of where it comes from.

To forgive even criminal acts is not to take a position of permissiveness. You can forgive a person without tolerating his or her behavior or exposing yourself to it. Forgive the pain, but don't forget the lesson. A prison structure for criminals protects society. Avoidance is appropriate if disrespectful behavior cannot be corrected. Walking alone in New York City at night is inviting difficulty. Even Zen monks oust disrespectful students. If your parents still think that you, as an adult, don't handle yourself well, that's their problem and not yours. If you actually become disrespectful, it's your problem. Forgive yourself for not previously knowing about the Big Picture. Forgive your parents for not knowing.

4. NO PREACHING: Telling others about the things you've learned when they don't want to hear them is a waste of time. To preach is to be fearful that they won't get the message. Some people refuse to accept the Big Picture. They don't want to hear about Lone Ranger/Helpless Victim patterns. They may, eventu-

ally, die within the limitations of their awareness. They may die in a state of denial, attachment or addiction. Practice consistently on your own awareness, but don't become a victim by trying to fix their reticence and fear of intimacy.

Do not try to become "The Master" for them. Caretaking never works. People cannot be manipulated into deeper level awareness, and they will be resentful if you try. They must have had enough pain in their lives to consistently seek it on their own. Appropriate intervention is, of course, useful and often productive. Repeated intervention is a waste of time. Do not use the word "codependency" on your loved ones. The word itself is mysterious and has connotations of sickness. Strive for balanced observation of others. Recognize what they do well and what they need work on. None of us is 100-percent well or 100-percent sick.

5. SERIOUS BOUNDARY MANAGEMENT: Remain serious about boundaries at all times. If others try to behave in dependent ways with you, (i.e., blame, anger, relentless crying and refusal to become self-responsible) *you will pay dearly for listening too long.* Place some distance in that kind of relationship. The diminished verbal or physical intimacy might be the kendo swat that will force them to think. Your apparent disinterest, your silence, could be a kindness. This is especially important for adults who must handle relationships with unenlightened parents or children. Time out can work for those of any age.

6. MIRROR FEELINGS: Don't be a receptacle for cathartic feelings of others. Instead, mirror them back: "You're continuously crying." "What do you intend to do about your situation?" "You repeatedly call me to ask for advice, but do nothing." "You're angry. I'm not, and I've been careful to be respectful."

Listen, but don't listen for too long. It *will* pull you down. You're not there as a receptacle for other people's feelings — you're not the city dump.

7. BECOME A QUIET MODEL: Visualize yourself as a model for others. You are, in fact, a model, so behave like one. If you're angry, others will be. If you whine and fuss, others will. If you posture yourself as an expert your associates will also. But, if you are consistently working on wellness, others will be turned in that direction, as well. If you make a mistake and are disrespectful, apologize. More responsibility will ultimately come to you if you *behave* responsibly.

FEELINGS

For years, our "mental health" model has been primitive and victim-oriented, focusing on "get your feelings out" or "say how you're feeling." It can easily become a scapegoat model, whereby you seek out those who treated you wrong. From that "traditional" perspective, you are well adjusted if you "emote." It's a remnant of the old cathartic theory from the late 1800s. The worst meeting I ever attended was when a group of psychiatrists, psychologists and social workers sat down in a group to "share" their feelings. Sheer madness ensued. It's like the old notion behind the development of breakfast cereals: Eat your bran and that daily evacuation will cure everything!

Let's now take a closer look at the feelings process and get more specific:

1. TOO MUCH OR TOO LITTLE: Lone Rangers do need to identify feelings in the recovery process. But the danger is that they will become unzipped and remain unzipped, placing themselves in a victim role. To *identify* feelings does not mean that you must continuously *express* them to everyone. Expressing feelings doesn't make you more responsible. It makes you appear irresponsible unless you are involved in a *specific therapeutic* setting with a plan to *use* the feelings for self-discovery and to manage them yourself.

Helpless Victims are already feelings-oriented. They are hurt, angry, sad, offended and will tell you quickly how bad it is. They must be also be tasked with *responsibly handling* their feelings, rather than *expressing* them. One woman cried to a therapist for four years before she came to see me. After she had been in treatment with me for a while, I told her we weren't going to repeat that experience. She began to improve, but in group sessions, regularly told long, unhappy stories about how badly she had been taken advantage of in recent life experiences with men. After several interventions, I ultimately asked her to leave the group for three months. The group had enabled her to continue expressing feelings without taking responsible action. Her victimhood had become their entertainment. She understood. I had more respect for her strength than she had for herself. She came back stronger and more determined and is now happily married after feeling for years that she would always be a victim.

2. BALANCE: Simply expressing feelings in social situations or in business isn't balanced. It's passive. It's weak. Feeling without reflection is out of balance. In therapy and in life, balanced remarks are objective: "Here's what you're doing well, and here's what you need to work on." Positive and negative. It's important to place the emphasis on *using* your feelings to internally *understand* your problem, instead of simply passively permitting the expression of feelings. To *process* feelings is to discover and objectively connect their significance with your recovery . It is not to blow them out and "get rid of them" for passive "feedback." In my groups, I have an imaginary buzzer which we all have fun with it. It's my group "cosmic horn." Anyone can honk it when he or she sees the speaker drifting off into denial or the repetitive whine of victimhood. One time, an executive related the following story:

> "The in-house lawyer came right into my office. He was hot and started giving me hell about my consultation with an out-of-house lawyer. I stopped him right there and said, '*I have a problem* with you coming in here like this.'
>
> 'Furthermore,' I said calmly, 'as executive VP I can consult whoever I wish. If you want

to schedule a meeting with the president to discuss this, I'd be happy to.' (So far, so good).

Then I said, 'I want you to know that I think you're a unmitigated SOB, and I've been angry with you for months.'"

He was fussing. HONK! HONK! He got into his feelings and lost his self-management. Additionally, he gave the in-house lawyer much ammo for gossip. He lost his composure and victimized himself. Our group horn helped him focus on his victimhood and lack of balance.

3. FEELINGS AND MANIPULATION: Expressing feelings is an attempt to manipulate through guilt. There are four steps in that well-known book *The One Minute Manager* that are designed to handle the errant employee with dispatch. Step number three in the one minute criticism is: tell them how you feel. HONK! How you feel has nothing to do with their job. It might be temporarily effective as a tool for manipulation. But in the end, it will only create problems. All the employees need from you, quite simply, is a moment of your time to give them balanced remarks such as, "This was done well. This was done poorly." Those remarks are aligned with a balanced natural order. You aren't begging or pleading or acting hurt. You're just taking time to tell the employees about the way things are — about your parameters, your requirements, your garden and their garden.

4. TREATMENT PROBLEMS: So many support groups become regressive victim groups with the pour-out-your-feelings agenda. They are dumps that encourage an *illusion* of recovery. No one gets better from *sharing*. No one gets better from *feedback*. If you *know* how you feel, why go to group and burden everyone else? Groups are opportunities for *self-discovery* and for defining *responsible action*. If feelings come up, they are opportunities for *self-awareness*, not opportunities for being taken care of and loved. Groups aren't there to "love" crying people into wellness. It won't work. It

encourages entitlement. They make people think, "I have a right to remain in pain."

Sharing can be helpful since it might diminish entitlement. Feedback can add dimensions to the Big Picture. But *responsible action* and responsible self-care are the hallmarks of balanced recovery. While expressing feelings, keep your self-observing mind in gear. Don't take the opportunity of apparent permission to behave irresponsibly by dumping. A litany of long-suffering details can be dispensed with and replaced by a statement of the problem and some self-suggested action plan. An angry argument quickly becomes a whine. Groups don't like victims. A group for balanced remarks can offer transcendent Big Picture observations to support the responsibility of recovery action.

THE GROUP: "FAMILY" BUSINESS

I've heard it said by some that "this business is like a family." And the business may, in fact, be run by a family. But, it is asking for big trouble to consider any business as being a "family." Such a business is often plagued by too much emphasis on parenting and not enough on adult business. Besides, families are often more disrespectful with each other than with business associates. You don't *need* another "family." Balance is far more important. The family connotation is one of being taken care of. Most family businesses are too vertical; they are paternalistic by description. It even sounds entitled. Just call it "the business." Treat family like respected business partners and forget the childhood connotations. The "family business" can easily become just another Teddy Bear. Respect is the bottom line. If, on the other hand, "like a family" means treating each other with a high level of respect, balanced remarks, and common courtesy, then the "family" comment does make sense.

WHY COLD CALLING

Do what you fear to do and the fear will die.
Ralph Waldo Emerson

Healing your self-esteem problems is *not just a conceptual mental operation*. It is not just an affect, a feeling release. Self-esteem healing takes place through the practice of *doing* in the real world. *Healing takes place through responsible action.* As you practice doing and taking responsible action verbally and behaviorally, you will grow in your self-confidence. Responsible action is process-focused, not content-limited. As Tom Peters said in *In Search of Excellence:* "Ready, Fire, Aim." Fire responsibly wherever you aim. Get into action. Don't keep waiting for the right conceptual target. With balanced, creative action, the target often appears (The Theory of Circumvential Direction).

Through cold calling, you will be exposed to the pressures and pulls of other individuals and groups. Through that exposure, you will learn of your own vulnerabilities, your own attachments and your own illusions. It is your opportunity, as it was with Gandhi, to live in other villages — to live in the context of different relationships. It is a balance of respectful commitment to old relationships and an openness to the formation of new ones.

As you proceed, you will come to know yourself. But you will also come to know how others think and behave. When your vision comes to penetrate their patterns as well as your own, you'll be fighting fewer battles.

Plan for what is difficult while it is easy, do what is great while it is small. The most difficult things in the world must be done while they are still easy, the greatest things in the world must be done while they are still small. For this reason, sages never do what is great and this is why they can achieve that greatness.
Sun Tzu
Chinese Warrior-Philosopher

10

Staying On
The Train:

Specific Action Over Time

*Nothing in the world can take the place of
persistence. Talent will not; nothing is more
common than unsuccessful men with talent.
Genius will not; unrewarded genius is almost a
proverb. Education will not; the world is full of
educated derelicts. Persistence and determination
alone are omnipotent.*

Calvin Coolidge
30th U.S. President

THERE IS AN OLD BLACK SPIRITUAL recently rerecorded
by Rod Stewart which says: "People get ready, there's a
train a'comin. You don't need no ticket, just get on board."
It told of the freedom train that took blacks from their en-
slavement in the South to freedom up North. It is a song
remarkably relevant even today. There is a metaphoric
train, a path of self-realization and self-awareness, that
awaits anyone, anywhere, at any time. You probably won't
look around for it unless you're depressed, hurting or just
fed up. It's probably inevitable that you will, at some point,
become frustrated with your relationships. Maybe you already are. The question is what do you intend to *do* about
it?

Likely, you'll respond in your programmed, diacritic, way a few more times, reaching new heights of creativity in denial and manipulation. And when it doesn't work your way, you'll start lying to yourself about it, telling yourself you aren't scared and that gratification and distraction can work for you. And if you practice such delusion and dishonesty with yourself, it is only a matter of time before you'll be lying to others.

In the recovery field, this is called relapse. Melodie Beattie calls it "recycling." You soon find yourself back in defensive patterns. Likely, you'll be a little worse off than you were previously, because you're more determined to make your unbalanced methods work. But, when defensive activity is used in the context of the natural order, your original pain always comes back — in spades. That one is guaranteed. The positive side is that you have a brand new chance to learn from the pain of attachment.

So in your pain, you look around one more time and chance upon the train of self-awareness. It's a train that goes up the Big Picture Mountain, up near the River of No Return. If you practice Deep Recovery, there's no going back to the old you. It's too painful to do. But once you decide to look at the higher order and ride the train, you're faced immediately with another problem. It seems difficult to pay attention and stay on track, because the world of illusion and distraction tries to lure you off the path through every step of the journey.

RELAPSE: ALTERNATIVES

You will find that your self-awareness freedom train of detachment regularly makes stops at various stations along the way. The stops are specifically designed to seduce you off the train again. New environments and new relationship experiences constantly present new opportunities for self-delusion and unbalanced gratification.

You may jump on the train in search of a way to understand a painful dependency relationship in your adult life, only to find on down the time line that you've fallen off the train again and have become emotionally dependent on your own children. You may climb aboard thinking you have an alcohol problem and get off the train at the station of free cocaine.

The opportunities to get off are always there. Any gratification can seduce you into a delusion. This is especially true in relationships. These gratification stations offer many opportunities for fixed emotional attachments — for pure distraction. They aren't to be confused with the simple, balanced connections of exchange between recovering individuals. Instead, they refocus your attention on gratification and feeling good. They'll keep you focused on "needs," on dependency and counterdependency patterns. And, they can make you feel so comfortable that they encourage you to lay over — to stay there over time.

There's an interesting thing about these illusion stations of gratification: Each gratification is connected to others by comfortable, laser-fast modules. The modules travel faster than the freedom train and are thought-controlled. They can zip you from one illusion station to another as quickly as you can think about it. No effort is required — but, there is a high price with this ride. On the freedom train, you have to give up your illusions. On this one, you give up your life — your own moments of being alive, of connecting with reality as it truly is. Gratification stations can draw you into a death-like stasis. Because if you aren't living fully, you're dying. Yes, you can stop the recovery train anywhere. But if you stop off in gratification, always remember the price. And remember that some people literally destroy their lives in their efforts to cope with the fear of dying. They will change gratifications to avoid the fear of change.

Keep in mind that it's not all work on the recovery train. It isn't all seriousness and problems. You *can* also play. You can laugh and have a wonderful time. The people there are seeking balance and are involved in the self-change process. The company is interesting. They are all, in a way, both teachers *and* students. Some may be a bit confused. But they practice "beginner's mind" and are delightfully aware of the passing scene. They aren't boring because they aren't repetitive. Oh yes, some do get off the train occasionally. Sometimes, they come back wiser — and sometimes you never see them again.

You, too, will get off the train a few times at one station or another. Relationship stations offer the greatest opportunity for unbalanced gratification. The temptation of being an expert, or the safety of being taken care of, can keep us preoccupied for years ... indeed, for a lifetime. Two other popular stops these days are "money" and "power." One of the remarks made by each station master is "a little bit won't hurt you." And it is true. One little bit of anything isn't the problem. The problem is that in making the decision to yield to gratification, you forget what you've learned. When you get off, you may temporarily forget your painful lessons. You may forget to pay attention.

Your past record of relationship pain is all you have going for you. Your pain may seem like a burden, but it's really your own personal lesson plan. If you review carefully how you've made it this far, you'll see how instructive the pain has been for you. Coming to terms with your own pain, and understanding its usefulness, will keep you from stopping too long at illusion stations.

COMPARISONS: MEN AND WOMEN

One of the most subtle forms of self-delusion is the stop at the station of comparisons. In Chapter Three, we began to see how language reduces the variables and makes life deceptively simple. Language can drive us us into polarities and disconnections before we even think about it. Our everyday language encourages the formation of preconceptions and comparisons. It actually colors the tone before the "discussion" begins.

However:

There is light in the darkness;
Do not look with dark seeing eyes
There is darkness in the light;
Do not look with light seeing eyes
                    Taisen Deshimaru
                    Zen Master, martial artist

To be free to choose, one must be free of comparisons. With comparisons, the emotional choice is already made. There is much significance, therefore, to the current array of "women's literature" and the new wave of "men's literature." It's humorous that women and men think they are so different when the popular titles could easily be rewritten in the reverse. Consider *Women Who Hate Men and the Men Who Love Them*. Or, how about *Men Who Love Too Much*. You see how ridiculous it is? The concept of "women's problems" and "men's problems" keeps people polarized in a delusion that separates them from the solution they seek.

It's primitive to think that just because the sexual equipment is different that we have different goals for ourselves as human beings. Special "men's and women's" issues brings "special needs." Sounds like entitlement to me. Is the love that women want different, in any way, from the love men want? Women want respect, appreciation and commitment. Men want the same things. The rest of the "need" trimmings create a sense of victimhood and a series of special requests. If men and women could love *themselves* more and demand less, they would be happy partners.

Comparisons are an invidious form of dualistic thinking which imply that "I'm unique, I'm different," etc. In the next breath comes the reasons for the entitlement, an empty effort at retrenchment in "needs." The "men's issues, women's issues" differences become an overt manifestation of the very separation each wishes to avoid. Such specialized need perspectives actually program partners for separation. They are saying repeatedly, in one way or another, that "I'm special." The remark suggests separate, different action for men and women. "Do more for me than you do for yourself." The remark is aimed at changing how your partner takes care of you.

And your partner's likely response? "If you're so different, perhaps you need someone who's also different — someone special, like you. Farewell."

A woman who repeatedly remarks about her differences suggests that she may be so different that she's beyond understanding or corrective action on his part. And what are other women going to say to her partner? "Gee, we have so many things in common. I'm interested in what you're interested in." Now, who do you think he will want to spend time with?

Most of us intuitively know from our work experience and involvement with groups that we can't pull that "I'm special" business without getting a serious hatchet job done on ourselves. What if that *Homo erectus* hunter turned to his hunting partner and said, "Can I share my special feelings and needs with you?" He'd probably be killed on the spot. But if "women's literature" keeps encouraging such polarities, can men be far behind? No wonder over 50 percent of marriages don't make it. Now, everyone has "feelings," and wants to be taken care of. If you don't understand or join in the fun, then you're "insensitive."

If you look for the diacritic differences, your "special needs," you will create separations. If you look for the commonality, the synchronistic similarity to the struggles that we all share, you will create *recovery partners*. If we *all* understand the larger problem, we can grow together as couples and families. We can free ourselves and others from the victimhood of need comparison. Our similarities are reassuring — our differences are the source of endless diatribe.

SEX

If everyone is so different and special, who can connect in the bedroom? Our sexual lives are often an expression of this disconnection in our search for specialness. Sex can be fun and play or it can be an illusory pathway to self-esteem and feeling better. It can be a happy exchange of affection, or it can be the ultimate manifestation of dependency in search for approval. If sex is constantly considered either a "big thing" or something to be avoided, then it's an unbalanced self-esteem barometer. Use sex as another lesson opportunity. Respect your partner's agenda without putting aside your own.

Incidently, let me go firmly on the record as recognizing that sex can be addictive and that sexual addiction exists. Those who don't believe that it can be addictive need to go for a long walk down the street of life. I know a male bisexual who is HIV positive with active AIDS. He is a sexual addict who has knowingly contributed to the probable deaths of many men and women. He was molested as a child and is now bisexually addicted. His sex is compulsive, destructive and out of control. Amazingly, he is in total denial about the consequences. He is victimizing himself and others through his compulsive need for gratification.

Any treatment program that treats only one addiction without addressing the others is setting people up for relapse. Denial in one dependency feeds denial in others. Denial of a sexual addiction feeds denial of other dependencies. Just because some people previously thought (reductionistically and categorically) that they were *only* alcoholics or *only* drug addicts, is no reason to not accept the interrelatedness of all dependencies now.

Sexuality must be freed from its connection with self-esteem, especially in these days when imprudent intercourse can be deadly. During the '60s, '70s and '80s, we became a society that believed in giving our companions reassurance by sleeping with them. Now, we have to let our friends handle their own self-esteem problems. No more sexual handshakes on the first date. Let's spend some time with our partners first, and see how they handle their lives. Let's see if they have any self-respect before we jump in seeking mutual approval through ministrations of sexual intimacy.

The intimacy sequence pattern in the past went from verbal, to physical and then to bonding. Then, as a frightened society ever seeking gratification, we switched it to physical, then verbal and who knows what's next?

Sex, like so much of life, has become a test — a test for approval. We want a grade. We want to know that we are adequate. "Are the breasts sufficient?" "Is the penis large enough?" "How about the motion or the verbalizations?" "How was it for you?" "Tell me about your orgasm." We think that if we can get into our partners' heads, we can find out if we're okay.

Often, the more sexually intimate we become, the more intensely we form attachments. Our need for approval intensifies, because we want to keep this person. But you can't keep anyone, anyway. So, why not start from a position of mutual self-respect and work into commitment, rather than beginning with sexual intimacy, implied commitment and then making subsequent efforts to work into self-respect?

RECOVERY PROGRAM OBSTACLES

Your "program" is the structure and discipline that you place in your own life for your continued effort at self-awareness. Your program is whatever personal structure works to help you stay on the train. If you don't have a personal structure, design one. Without a structure, you will remain adrift. Reading this book, or seeing someone in therapy once a week, is simply not sufficient to overcome relationship dependency/counterdependency patterns. Not that psychotherapy or reading this book won't help. Such aids will get you over some bumps, but they can hardly help you in the long run with the Big Picture. Working on the Big Picture requires an effort at paying attention all of the time. Through a schedule of personal development, you can see for yourself how you get on and off the train. With practice, the process becomes second nature.

On a cautionary note, there are certain potential recovery program obstacles that do exist within the "recovery" community. These potential obstacles may provide a faulty structure for your self-awareness activities. Like everything else we've talked about, nothing is all good or all bad. These problems can, through the tricks of language and your own misunderstanding, cause a person to go from a structure of *good* theory to *bad* life action.

UNCONDITIONAL LOVE

The concept of unconditional love is spiritually and transcendentally useful. The idea of accepting the similarity of problems throughout humankind, and of loving others in spite of their mistakes, is a goal worthy of consideration. It encourages forgiveness and accepts different levels of recovery awareness. It lets go of the past. The problem is that *operationally,* in practice, it often manifests itself as victimhood in action.

Unconditional acceptance should never be confused with *unconditional permission.* Unconditional love might be taken to mean that anyone can step on your squash. Many Helpless Victims inappropriately use the concept of unconditional love to rationalize their permissiveness. Through that concept, they continue to act out their victim position in the present. They want unconditional love from their mates, permission for their irresponsibility. They long for specialness and entitlement. Unconditional love encourages confusion in boundary management. It leaves too many issues wide open for debate.

Remember, this recovery process is very confusing to the uninitiated. We must keep our terms simple and clearly operational, lest we encourage further confusion and stasis. I suggest that we may *think* unconditional love/acceptance in our relationships, but that we regularly *live* in conditional relationships. All relationships are, in fact, operationally and functionally conditional. Unconditional relationships are unbalanced and have confused boundaries.

What is a woman, who has been married to four violent alcoholics, going to do with a term like unconditional love? Keep in mind that she's a "codependent," a dependent person. What will she do *operationally* with that term? She'll forgive them, of course. But she may miss her lesson! I say she should logically and emotionally *forgive* those husbands, but *learn* the lesson! The men were addicted and unenlightened. She, along with them, had lived in a dreamland. Now, it's time for her to assume responsibility. Operationally, she needs to decide to *never* accept alcoholism or abuse in her life again. That decision is based upon conditional love.

If you have a friend who is an alcoholic or a dependent, non-recovering person, the relationship is not going to work in the long run. Period. No debate. Strict conditions.

184 / DEEP RECOVERY

Your self-awareness program should set clear limits on victimhood and self-abuse. There should be no confusion in these matters. Now, if, for example, the guy you're dating is in solid recovery and working on himself consistently, it might work out. But if he goes to a meeting only occasionally, it simply doesn't count.

Ernest Hemingway said it very well: "Never confuse motion with action."

Decisive recovery action is more than going through the motions. The concept of unconditional love can keep you from taking self-protective *action*. It allows you to focus on the 10 percent that's workable and forget about the 90 percent that's completely impossible. Unconditional love is *unconditional* — it's a categorical trap.

Once a woman came tearfully into my office. Between sobs she said, "I've lost all of my children." During the years when they were very young, she had regularly taught them how to rationalize and enable their father's chronic alcoholism. "Your father is sick. He needs your kindness and understanding," she would tell them. "Always remember to be kind to your father. He needs your help."

Ultimately, she decided to protect herself and separated from him. In the divorce proceedings, she hired a friend, the church attorney, to represent her. Her husband hired a top-gun divorce lawyer and requested full custody of the children. At the hearing, the judge took the three children into his chambers and asked them which parent they wanted to live with. They remembered their lessons well. They all requested their father — he "needed" them.

Later, the father refused to allow her visits with the children. He made up lies and tortured her further by having the children write hateful letters to her. It was, for her, a fate worse than their deaths. She had loved her husband unconditionally. Unconditional thinking is unbalanced, categorical and self-destructive.

THE TRAP OF THE CHILD WITHIN

I've admitted to Peninsula Hospital's dependency programs, several women who had come with excess baggage from other treatment centers around the country. They literally arrived with their own stuffed Teddy Bears. In other "codependency" programs, they had been taught to "nurture their child within" by carrying a stuffed animal. And so, by talking baby talk to their Teddy Bear, they attempted to nurture themselves.

It's true that the "child within" concept can provide a latticework upon which to structure and review one's past. But, for some it can become a serious liability which inhibits and may, ultimately, forestall the recovery process. Consider these points:

1. The recovery process involves the development of responsibility in the *current* relationships of your adult life. To emphasize the development of a childlike persona can freeze someone in the past. It's focus argues against work in the *present.*

2. Most people enter therapy with their childhoods already screaming loudly over their efforts to contain them. Their present conflicts are a direct expression and representation of their childhood traumas. Why create additional regressive and childlike representations that require further attention? It only adds to the regression that's already present.

3. A childlike persona is more vulnerable and less able to balance life in an adult manner. Adult boundary setting is less likely to be accomplished if you have become your child within.

4. The best target population for the child within concept, the Lone Rangers (who are defensively locked into cognitive perfectionism), will be resentful when tasked with becoming a victim. They dislike victims. On the other hand, they are cooperative when shown instead how they can seek balance. You don't have to be a child to have feelings.

5. The victims of the world are already locked into the past and the discharge of their feelings. *It's counter-*

productive to give theatrical permission to act out their childhood feelings more dramatically than they already have. There are too many secondary gains.

6. The goal of therapy is balance in your current life. The goal of the child within process argues, at times, against the recovery process. It encourages self-caretaking and nurture, rather than balanced self-management. And caretaking is where the problems started.

Those who have become frozen in their struggles with the child within are unhappy victims. They become stuck in victimhood and in carrying their Teddy Bears. They use their "recovery" as a means of obtaining pity from others. Their "recovery" becomes an illness, with attendant secondary gains that are fed by the recovering community. The illness becomes cemented by "recovery." *They* become the object of caretaking by others.

I suggest we begin to consider an alternative: The Adult Within. By tasking ourselves with becoming self-managed adults, we can use our growth and strength to handle our troubled pasts. We can remain in the present and achieve balance. And through self-mastery, our self-esteem will be enhanced, rather than diminished through the addition of a new focus.

Lone Rangers and Helpless Victims can see their recovery task more clearly and put the past back in the past. They can let go of their previous victim preoccupations. Their early defensive patterns were already childlike. To become dependent on a part of yourself is still a form of dependency. Recovery is freedom from self and the delusions of self. The dependent, insecure self looks for more dependency operations wherever they can be found. And, with many recovery staffs encouraging Teddy Bears and cooing over regressive behavior, it can be a serious trap. No wonder that some recovering people become dependent upon "treatment."

ZIPPED AND UNZIPPED

Recently, a number of intensive, five- to ten-day, "codependency" programs have independently burst upon the national treatment scene. These are programs that can be helpful or damaging, depending on some of the "therapeutic" practices employed. Some patients, having developed profound reactions to these programs and the severity of the regressive and destructive practices, have subsequently been referred to our treatment team for hospitalization.

It is surprising to me, having been originally trained as a psychoanalyst, how many people in the recovery field are using outdated psychoanalytic theory as a foundation for recovery. They disdain analysts and the psychoanalytic process, and yet use tools that psychoanalysts themselves, discontinued before the turn of the century (1892).

These therapeutic techniques are based upon the old cathartic theory which Freud himself argued against. That theory is based upon the assumption that if you recreate and release the old affects (feelings), you will be healed. This is like the Milk of Magnesia of mental health. Catharsis, as a primary treatment modality, went out with scream therapy and Dr. Green's advice to parents who wish to prevent their children from becoming transsexuals: "Walk naked in front of your children."

The new term for cathartic efforts, "Psychodrama," is a powerful tool that may occasionally be successfully used in *specific* treatment situations. But, it's use *as a standard operating procedure* is not to be recommended. The problems associated with catharsis and psychodrama are:

1. It's "powerful" because it's *regressive*. At its worst, it may encourage role playing (a dependent trait to be discouraged) and public displays of victimhood (which victims use to seek secondary gains).

2. Psychodrama may encourage the split between the "perfect" charismatic and manipulative therapeutic staff, who omnipotently orchestrate the scene, and the recovering "sick" patients who are encouraged to let it all out.

3. The past, as with "the child within", may remain operationally disconnected from the patients' present daily lives. In fact, the dramatic regression may have little, if any, operational value in their current recov-

ery programs.

4. Psychodrama, designed for emotional relief, in some respects adds insult to injury. By reliving the trauma, it is sometimes magnified.

5. Most importantly, psychodrama leaves behind this therapeutic message: "Just let it all out. Cry. Be angry and fuss — you'll get better." This attitude recreates a victim role in life. Catharsis is *not* the answer. Self-management *is*.

6. Psychodrama's emphasis on the past doesn't work congruently with chemical dependency recovery, which is focused on the present, one day at a time. It leaves recovering individuals mixed up regarding their problems (Is it codependency, or is it alcoholism? Is it past or present pain?)

7. The patient can remain unzipped and frozen in the past.

8. The reality of the past is distorted by layers of denial. The reality of present relationship circumstances is less subject to distortion.

Answer this question: As a Helpless Victim, would you go away for five to ten days to express yourself *even more* than you already have? If you are a Lone Ranger and you haven't dealt with your feelings, you may feel victimized as you go with the pace of the therapist rather than finding your own tempo. Psychodrama, at times, can be an act of therapeutic anxiety and impatience, a trick to force issues out of patients that would come out naturally in time, anyway.

In my work in the field of "codependency recovery," I have seen specific examples of each of these difficulties. Some psychodrama patients get caught up in role playing. Others get caught up in the past and feel they were worse off for having been through the experience.

A particularly deteriorated woman, who needed hospitalization, worked as a professional in the field of codependency recovery. She had previously been hospitalized and "walked through" a series of psychodrama events, including three very traumatic rapes that had occurred during her adolescence. By going through that process, she felt she had been serially raped again. Her psychic reality was one of being mentally re-raped.

Another patient relived a traumatic childhood with her father and a particular incident of verbal abuse. She entered the in-patient program at Peninsula arrested in fear and unable to free herself from that traumatic moment in the past. Clutching her Teddy Bear, she was vainly trying to manage the trauma by nurturing her "inner child."

It took a week of reassurance and support on the in-patient unit to convince these women that we wouldn't use psychodrama in our treatment program. As it turned out, the predominant effort in our treatment was in helping them to manage their previous treatment. Only then, could we align each patient with her traumatic past so that she could effectively *use* it to gain lessons for her present life.

To be balanced, psychodrama can be a useful practice run. Done appropriately, it can serve the process of unzipping and zipping up. It can put closure on the past. It's not *all* wrong, but certain aspects do have the potential for causing problems. Some positive uses for psychodrama include the following:

1. Psychodrama can be used to rework the past and do what was left undone back then. This is not passive catharsis, but mastery.

2. A person can, through serial roles on a time line, experientially pull events together to correct them within the context of a current difficulty. In this way, past difficulties can be felt, connected to current difficulties and restructured in a healing way, *with an emphasis on balance.* The support of the group in this scenario is one of "you can manage it," rather than "you can feel it."

3. Current difficult living situations can be affectively reviewed and reworked in a balanced way using psychodrama as a restructuring process in the present. It's not only a tool for working with the past.

4. Therapists and patients, who are caught up in overemphasizing the past through psychodrama, can use the technique to balance their activities on a time

line. Balance the psychodrama process by including current conflicts and current life situations.

The responsibility of a balanced program is to help patients slowly unzip (discover repressed feelings) and then zip back up (use the feelings as a guide for responsible action). Being able to zip back up is as much a part of recovery as unzipping. Zipping up for responsible action cannot be accomplished with a treatment technique of simple reassurance while the patient is in pain. Reassurance encourages victimhood. It's a secondary gain for feeling bad. Through zipping up, you can develop a sense of mastery of your own past lessons and integrate them with your present reality. Healing is an affective *and* cognitive process, not just affective.

THE STRUCTURE FOR YOUR PROGRAM

1. The recovery process involves mind, body and spirit. Leave out any one of these aspects, and you'll have a harder time of it. Many in recovery work only one or two aspects of a full recovery program. They resist the surrender to discipline. They avoid self-responsibility. Consistency brings the fastest rewards. Your recovery structure should include each of the following activities regularly:
   A. Work on the MIND
      - Specific reading (see appendix). This is mandatory.
      - Participation in discussion groups.
      - Individual and/or group psychotherapy with a trained therapist who will not undermine a *total* recovery effort.
   B. Work on the BODY
      - Regular aerobic exercise (to target heart rate) at least three times a week. This is mandatory. Smoking and recovery don't mix.
      - Regular participation in a sports-related activity that may or may not be in conjunction with your cardiovascular work out. Such activities might include fishing, horseback riding, weight-lifting, bird watching or hiking.

I feel so bad"). The cure arrives through thinking. It ignores the biology of recovery, the "disease" model. By emphasizing the past, it may encourage rationalization and avoidance of current responsibility. It encourages interpretation as a defense.

Because of this dispute, some chemical dependency treatment programs have been largely behavioral/educational and not sufficiently psychological. Others have leaned toward the psychological without sufficient emphasis on behavioral change and assumption of personal responsibility for recovery.

Traditionally, such polemic units have had to be geographically separated from each other in treatment facilities because each staff has different philosophies and different methods for recovery. Disputes commonly arose regarding patient care. There are now many free-standing chemical dependency centers that have one type of treatment and psychiatric units with another. Each type of staff feels comfortable with its delivery of service and its own polemic philosophy. But in the end, many patients remain confused.

As a resolution to the conflict, I suggest that we combine the best of the two approaches and encourage comprehensive, corrective action. We know that the past *is* relevant. Furthermore, psychological dependency patterns are relevant. But since psychological patterns have been there since the beginning of language, there's no one to blame. Recognition of the psychological patterns (insight) can encourage responsibility and detachment. Recognition of these psychological dependency patterns can encourage chemical dependency recovery. Psychological dependency *and* chemical dependency programs are both reality-oriented and based on *action* (not only thinking).

Recovery from psychological dependency and chemical dependency *both* require *ongoing awareness* and an evolving sense of *self-responsibility*. There is no termination, no end point to self-management. The recovery concepts are easily understandable and teachable. They overlap. Relapse in either type of program brings the same consequences — more dependency, more pain and further self-victimization.

The obvious conclusion is that psychiatric and chemical dependency recovery programs can be successfully integrated, while they can also maintain their respective autonomy. There are many opportunities for integration and sharing of skills and treatments in the recovery process.

TREATMENT PROGRAM OBSERVATIONS: STEAMROLLER THERAPY

Treatment programs that encourage shouting, anger, sarcasm and snide remarks as part of their treatment are primitive, sick programs. Just as you can't be hugged into recovery, you can't be criticized into it. These programs are unhealthy families that teach their children to bully. Nevertheless, such unbalanced, angry and punitive behavioral programs are still the vogue for chemical dependency treatment. In those programs, if patients have any denial, the staff may infantilize them and berate them. They may humiliate them and mock them. This is caveman mentality and behavior. Ironically, this kind of staff often clings to the biological disease model in an effort to expiate the patient's guilt ("It was my disease that did that"). Yet, patients *must* assume responsibility for their actions in order to change them. Strict behavioral programs encourage patients to look at the past *only* after six months to one year of sobriety. Sooner than that, they say, a person will relapse. Oftentimes, such a delay is recommended because the "codependency" treatment is based on profound regression through psychodrama. Yet contradictorally, many of those same treatment programs include built-in fourth step work (from AA's 12-Step Programs) that indeed involves careful *past* psychological inventory and review. They're actually doing *psychological work* in the programs, but think of it as only *disease model behavioral work.*

THE CHEMICAL DEPENDENCY — RELATIONSHIP DEPENDENCY CONNECTION

Let's permit ourselves to do what many of us already do, anyway. We can think of two or three things at the same time. We can drive and talk at the same time. Humans *can* have a biologically-inherited disease and have an associated psychological dependency at the same time. In fact, we can have several psychological dependencies: alcohol, cocaine, sex, work, food and relationships can all be problems for one person at the same time. Why work with only the alcohol and cocaine problems for six months to a year, and allow the denial to exist in all the other dependencies? Denial feeds denial. Denial of sexual dependency will feed the denial of chemical dependency. The patient will likely go back to chemicals to handle the pain of non-recovery in the other areas of their lives.

"But," you may hasten to inquire, "won't that kind of dual emphasis feed the denial of their chemical dependency problem?" The answer is no — not if we can see the interrelationship of addictions. Not if we repeatedly emphasize *the simple fact that without primary chemical dependency sobriety and recovery, no other recovery is possible.* If your brain can't work, we can't talk to it.

At Peninsula Hospital, we start with one to two weeks of first-step work including clear, consistent focus on the chemical dependency problem. Then, we look for denial wherever else it resides — in relationships, most importantly. If this hospitalization represents one of several relapses and denial of relationship dependency is present, we may start the person immediately in relationship dependency work, as well. We feel that relationship work is very important. It's done anyway with family weekends and family focus meetings. So, why not do it correctly and responsibly instead of waiting six months to a year? Why not integrate it into the existing program? It doesn't put anyone "in their head," if it *fits with and parallels the action oriented recovery program of chemical dependency.*

Such a process *will* put them in their head if they look for *blaming explanation and excuses* from the past. But if they look at the past as *painful learning opportunities for responsible recovery action,* it will fit right in with their 12-Step Recovery Program. Pain brings insight. Insight is the beginning of self-responsibility. Following the RAPIDS concept, we can see how our fears of reality encourage at-

tachments to chemicals and relationships. Subsequent
pain can give us insight to understand that these attachments don't work. We can use the pain to help detach
from old patterns and take specific responsible action. It is
your *pain* that will constantly remind you to detach, not
your *program*.

The review of *all* contributory problems is a fresh, balanced, common-sense approach to all of our dependencies.
One recovery feeds the other. Denial is fair game wherever it rears its ugly head. Let us patiently begin to evolve
from fundamentalist, categorical conceptualizations and
take responsible, comprehensive, healing action in our personal recovery programs. Let us behave with each other
in ways that we all respect. If recovery means yelling at
each other, who wants to recover? Let's make the balanced
recovery model more practically available in everyday life,
and begin working with all dependencies in the early
months of treatment.

Recovery programs should teach and process as many
separate dependency issues as possible for the brief time
people have in formal treatment. One reason that insur-
ance companies have encouraged reductions in chemical
dependency programs is that they hear education. They
don't hear pain. If patients' private lives aren't explored
during treatment, they will surely be set up for relapse
down the line.

Many chemical dependency programs rigidly attempt to
deal with relationship dependencies in a variety of ways:
no visits, no phone calls, etc. But, if the patients don't
have contact with loved ones, the therapists often won't
have that contact, either. So, the *family* remains out of recovery. It's up to the therapists to moderate, to balance as
much as possible, the friend/family interaction portion of
the program. And yes, some chemically dependent individuals do need more time to heal. Thirty days in-house
may sometimes not be enough.

The recovery process cannot stand above modern advances in psychopharmacology. Many reach an impasse in
recovery due to concurrent biological depression or bipolar
disorder (manic-depressive disorder). It's most ironic that

on the one hand, some recognize the inherited disease of chemical dependency while, on the other, they reject the inherited disease of depression.

Antidepressant medications and lithium are not addictive substances. Of course, given too quickly and too vigorously, they may indeed cause a temporary, unpleasant mind-altering experience. But that particular problem doesn't make them counterproductive to recovery. Given carefully, in conservative dosages with an eye on each person's *biochemical individuality,* they can be life-saving.

The negative feelings about psychopharmacologic agents must be reserved for addictive substances such as benzodiazapines (Ativan, Librium, Xanax and Valium), codeine and other opiates. *These* are the medications that contribute to depression and encourage relapse.

For medication consultation, there are an increasing number of psychiatrists and other physicians who are addiction specialists, certified by the American Society for Addiction Medicine (ASAM). They can be contacted at 12 West 21st Street, New York, N.Y. 10010 (212-206-6770). These individuals are more likely to be aware of the variety of psychotropic medications that can assist or deter the recovery process.

FEELINGS IN FAMILY THERAPY

On a final note about programs and family interaction, the treatment community in general should, in my opinion, rethink its whole approach to "feelings." So much of the family interaction portion of many programs fosters an *exchange of feelings* as though that activity will foster recovery. But the activity of feeling exchange can often encourage blame and guilt. I strongly suggest that we shift the healing emphasis to *responsibilities* rather than *feelings.* Feelings are important building blocks for future responsibilities, but they are not an end in themselves and don't necessarily contribute to ongoing family recovery.

Both family and patient should seek responsible, enlightened recovery action, rather than seeking change through exchange and expression of feelings. The family must responsibly look at its own recovery and dependency patterns in an effort to set up a gridwork of balanced self-awareness throughout the family recovery group. Families can't expect to manipulate their chemically dependent loved ones into recovery through feelings (anger or sadness) and guilt when manipulation is itself a primary symptom of dependency.

This advanced Deep Recovery dependency awareness and recovery model can also have many implications of usefulness beyond formal treatment programs. Certainly there are possibilities for its application in dependency or addiction prevention and in self-esteem education wherever these issues are discussed. This basic recovery self-management model could easily be taught in schools through health, self-esteem or self-development programs.

Let's all make a renewed effort to make recovery more interesting and more positive — not tedious, polemic and overwhelming. The train, the path to recovery, requires constant vigilance. But by staying alert, we need not feel that we must limit our vision. These two apparently different treatment philosophies can work synergistically, *if* we can seek the common ground. There, we can all have the opportunity for recovery.

The Deep Recovery Balance Process is present in every aspect of our human existence. It will have great application wherever people suffer in emotional pain or ignorance.

The train is always coming. You don't need a ticket, but you must work to stay on board. As you travel, you will feel more like teaching others, and you will feel less negative. With practice, you will automatically find yourself staying more alert. In time, the journey will become less tedious and provide fewer surprises.

Over the time of your travels, persistence and determination will reveal the Big Picture connections — connections that go beyond the limitations of theory.

11

Basic Lessons:

Recovery Leads To Leadership

An adventure is only an
inconvenience rightly considered.
                    G. K. Chesterton
                    English novelist

Men who love wisdom
should acquaint themselves
with a great many particulars.
                    Heraclitis, 500 B.C.
                    Greek philosopher

ONCE, AT A CONFERENCE, I HAD THE OCCASION to have an animated and entertaining conversation with an author in the mental health field who had recently published his first book. As the conversation drifted to a broader view of things, he remarked, "But of course, life has no meaning." This book is, if anything, a less than discursive argument with that remark.

It is my opinion that our lives are significant, that living a life can be a meaningful, fulfilling experience, and that learning the elemental lessons of life can encourage the most complete appreciation of that experience. Life's meaning is found in correct action. Correct action becomes meaningful experience. The guide to correct action is through the study of the *interconnection between particulars and universals*. The lessons of this developmental, connection process can be taught formally in high school, college, or wherever one trains for the real world. Or, they can be learned on a personal level from everyday experience. The only requirement? Awakening.

CONTENT — PARTICULARS

Most of the feelings and pain you've been working to get rid of can't be pushed away, excised, or successfully forgotten. It's all in the tapes of your past. But now you have some ways to begin to use these feelings and traumas as a positive, rather than a negative, force in your life.

So many of us have been stuck for years on particular points of content, specific points of pain: "Why did the boss say that?" "Why did she leave me?" "Why did I fall into that destructive relationship?"

So much of stasis and the repetition of illusion is based upon fixed, negative perceptions. Those negative perceptions and preoccupations can be placed upon either yourself, the outside world or both. The Lone Ranger perceives the world as negative. The victims perceive the negative to be within themselves. Each difficult event is mentally isolated. We keep going to the bathroom cabinet for Band-Aids to cover the wounds, because we are locked into the negative perception.

As you can see, however, the content of each event begins to blur when we look at the Big Picture. Each event has negative and positive attributes. Instead of working on events from the perspective of Small Mind in an effort to mentally manipulate our past or push problems away, we must switch our thinking to Big Mind which permits an acceptance and integration of the events of our lives. Each relationship event exists as a field of possibilities.

We've been twisting pieces of the puzzle, looking at the shapes of the edges instead of at the evolving background picture. The edges, the painful episodes of life, have little meaning as isolated diacritic events. The edges *and* the background complete the puzzle. Your content, your *particular* unique problems will be *different* from mine. But your problems have *characteristics* that are quite *similar* to mine and to everyone else's. Within the edges live usable, cohesive patterns. Life does have meaning.

These patterns are simple, obvious and easily understood. People unfamiliar with the recovery process can immediately grasp the principles and see their relevance in their own lives. We feel our lives are lost and without meaning when we find ourselves alone. We don't understand what our contribution to ourselves, or to humankind, can be. Further, we feel meaningless when we can't connect with the way the world actually works. A synonym for "meaningless" in this context is "futility." It's frustrating. If you can't see how things work, your efforts seem futile. That's because you're still chasing illusions — and, you know it.

As you take correct action, your past, your guilt, your shame and your pain can be usefully integrated into your developing value system. Your balanced value system evolves over time in recovery. Through your balanced, contributory values, you will find that leadership opportunities regularly come your way.

It is by paying attention to the details of your life, as they relate to the Balance Process and the Universal Design, that you will find meaning. Your life will not be meaningful with a limited, Small Mind view. Such a view will keep you lost in dependencies and gratifications which, in the end, will prove to be non-contributory, selfish and of limited value.

In review, let me remind you of six simple points that begin to summarize some of your personal lessons:

1. THE PAST: It is disquieting to be loved too much or not enough. Each of these feelings can leave us with a handicap of expectations. We humans share a common past, common expectations, common illusions. Our language sets us up to seek escape from the lessons of the past through avoidance and control.

2. GUILT: We are convinced we've done wrong. Others have an agenda for us which is impossible to fulfill. There's a sign on the wall of Narcotics Anonymous national headquarters that says "Guilt Kills." We have all, at one time or another, accepted blame for

the pain others feel when *their* expectations were not fulfilled. We are all natural caretakers. When unbalanced, we assume too much responsibility for others and not enought responsibility for ourselves. "Toxic shame" is actually a form of guilt.

3. SHAME: Shame leads us to recognize and change our disrespectful patterns, to make amends and apologize. What we didn't know because of our denial and blindness, we must forgive ourselves for. Shame can be an instrument of change for each of us. Through shame, we can correct ourselves. Mistakes are lessons. Ownership of our own lack of balance becomes self-corrective.

4. PAIN: It is a reminder of our desire to control and avoid. It's a message of attachment and victimhood common to humankind. Pain is inevitable, and it is, ultimately, useful for recovery.

5. CATCH-22 (The Rock and the Hard Place): No way out. This dilemma gives you the chance to seek the higher path through decisive, correct action. You realize now that you could have acted sooner when you saw it coming. Your discomfort over your indecisiveness will encourage more timely decisive action. Time repetitively reveals our patterns. We create our own traps. We seek out individuals who complement our unbalanced patterns.

6. VALUES: When you follow the path of honorable action, courage and honesty, you will feel better about your actions. Any other action causes loss of self-respect and shame. Values are a natural expression of deeper thought and meaningful action.

So many have difficulty with spiritual issues because they can't connect with a concept of God or of a higher power. They have had unbalanced dependency problems since childhood, and they project these patterns onto God. Their father was tyrannical, unloving and non-giving, so they expect God to be, as well. God seems so distant that it's impossible to connect.

If their mother was giving, loving and over-protective, they are disappointed by God. Their relationship with

God is based upon being protected from problems. So when problems occur, they are hurt and angry with God, because he didn't protect them. Their mother would have. Or, they might become religious fanatics who hope their prayers will protect them from reality. But God doesn't set people up. He doesn't rage. He isn't like your mother or father were. God transcends things and time. He is always there, waiting for you to wake up. He *is* the Natural Order, the larger system that transcends pain and limited vision.

Humans set themselves up for pain through their attachments to things and through avoidance and control. God patiently waits for us to recognize that we can't do it our way. He's there when we fall on our faces. Through acceptance of the Natural Order, we can come to accept the importance of spirituality and spiritual practice. We can connect with God and our fellow humans. Deep Recovery encourages a spiritually transcendent recognition of a universal system beyond human will.

PROCESS — UNIVERSALS

Ultimately, each of your particular relationship difficulties lead you to the Universal Process. Those specific points of light, each particular piece of the puzzle, can lead to the illumination of the entire Big Picture process. Each lesson reminds you of the process of the train ride, of the importance of small matters being handled well. We know that it's more than fish we're after. We're really beyond content. We're beyond single, specific events. Our correct attitude about inconvenience will connect the content, the process and the larger meaning, so that we will be able to make a positive contribution with our lives. The connections regularly reveal the larger order — the synesthetic process and the deeper opportunities in recovery.

For additional reading, you will see that I have included several books on the martial arts in the appendix. But the books aren't just about martial arts. They're about the integration of the self, the evolution of the self and the understanding of balance in the context of frightening reality.

The content and process of kendo, archery, karate and aikido all provide wide avenues of understanding for the Big Picture. In studying these activities, there is revealed an interconnectedness between the points, between the archer and target and between the motion of the sword, the mind, and the larger natural order. These books show how serious, even deadly adversaries can teach us about ourselves and about how the simple process of pouring tea or cutting wood can become a beautiful connection with the universal moment.

Several years ago, there was an editorial on the last page of Time Magazine entitled "The Benefits of a Good Enemy." It remarked on the value our enemies have for us as they hold our feet to the flame of correct action and push us to develop further. So it is with our most difficult relationships, our most painful life experiences. They can be our best teachers if we will only become willing students. All we need is a latticework upon which we can hang their remarks and our defenses. In the sword play, the tea ceremony, and the real carrying water of our relationships, we can come to see an illumination of the higher order. The very intensity of our relationships is, in fact, one of the best opportunities for self-development and enlightenment. But, we must push on with Big Mind and practice our awareness daily, or we will surely be lost in the single event, the content and the contact.

There is a martial arts school of swordmanship (kendo) called the "Sword of No Sword." Following many years of hard training with the sword, Tesshu, the master warrior, founded the school after a realization at 45 years of age. To paraphrase him:

> If there is no self, there is no enemy. No enemy means no sword. The past, present and future are all (an expression of your) one mind. The mind does not fix itself on the sword, but rather on all things. When the mind becomes fixed, it forms a reaction which is partly the reality and partly what we think reality is. When it becomes fixed, self and ego form illusions.

In that realization, Tesshu freed himself from thinking of the opponent's sword. His mind was free of the duality of opponents, free of the incumbrance of self and enemy. As he freed himself from thinking of the opponent's sword, he was further freed to react spontaneously. If his mind rested in attachment, for even a millisecond, on the enemy or the sword, he could be dead. In that millisecond he might, for example, become defensive, have a worry, or begin to think about a plan of attack. All of these take time. In sword play, as in life, thinking can kill you. You can die from comparisons, explanations and defensiveness.

The particular events of our lives lead to the universal natural order. After so many sword actions in relationships, it is time to be above swordplay. After so many words, it is time to be above words, to strive for a true freedom of your mind. It is time to be above men's and women's issues, above the polemics of recovery models. Codependency, the Lone Ranger and the Helpless Victim are disposable terms, merely gates leading to the old path that's been there since before time.

Seeking self-development, we must seek to let go of "therapy" and "self-development." We must search for our own path of responsible behavior. We must develop ownership of a practice that is our practice. We must go beyond "complete understanding" to correct action. Correct action needs no rationalization. It has a life of its own. It is obvious, yet not at all seeking to be obvious. It is free, but respectful of what others think, and brings order out of chaos or confusion. It is balanced, free of posturing or defensiveness. Correct action becomes a manifestation of leadership.

LEADERSHIP

Following the Way of Relationship Lessons will ultimately lead to leadership. To walk the middle way in balance, both connected and detached, brings new responsibilities. Responsibilities come automatically to balanced individuals. Over two thousand years ago, Sun Tzu outlined five qualities necessary for the leadership opportunities that will soon be presented to you as you grow in your practice. These qualities of leadership are a manifest form of values found through the practice of recovery. They are the same qualities we seek in our leaders today.

1. INTELLIGENCE: Seeing the larger order and the reactive dependency patterns gives the ability to plan and the knowledge to make changes effectively. To suggest action, everyone's patterns must be well understood. Big Mind thinking is free of the limitations of denial and unbalanced content perceptions. You won't get lost in the needs of individuals. Intelligent leadership is self-management and self responsibility in action.

2. CREDIBILITY: Rewards and consequences are consistently given out through the organization. There are no favorites. Problems are handled with dignity and dispatch. There is consistency in presence and personal behavior as well. Meetings begin and end on time. You accept your own responsibilities.

3. HUMANITY: There is love and compassion for others of all stations, from the highest to the lowest level of responsibility. There is no pretense or entitlement. There is no manifestation of ego above or below anyone. Relationships are balanced. Compassion is a manifestation of unconditional acceptance and the realization that we're all the same. There are no differences. We all have strengths and weaknesses. No one is absolutely negative or absolutely positive.

4. COURAGE: This is the manifest ability to act decisively without vacillation. Courage is associated with action. It's being able to go into the fray and behave respectfully, calmly and fearlessly. When you can cold call on each new reality — go towards it, not away from it — that's courage.

5. DISCIPLINE: Lines of respect and administrative authority are set for the organizational order and the responsibilities of others, as well as yourself. Decisive action taken against irresponsible or disrespectful behavior requires discipline. Clear boundaries and correct courtesy are necessary for all people. Con-

frontation of disrespectful behavior brings calm to the organization. Private criticism, public praise.

The boardroom, like the bedroom, is a place that may encourage petty rivalries and gossip. In every aspect of life, you will encounter the tension associated with the illusions and desires of others. Leadership offers no escape from these matters, only opportunities to use your growing awareness to manage larger situations effectively. Every aspect of life has its own lessons. As you continue to study these elemental truths and practice self-care, self-protection and respect for others, you will certainly become an Evolved Leader.

> *Evolved Individuals hold to the (Awareness)*
> *And regard the world as their Pattern.*
> *They do not display themselves;*
> *Therefore they are illuminated.*
> *They do not define themselves;*
> *Therefore they are distinguished.*
> *They do not make claims;*
> *Therefore they are credited.*
> *They do not boast;*
> *Therefore they advance.*
> *Lao Tzu*
> *Chinese Philosopher*

THIS BOOK

Now that you've started your path into the mountains and can see a bit more, I must make a slight confession. It is difficult, once you've started, to turn back. It is like that River of No Return. It has been my experience that you *can* turn back, but it's more painful to return to old ways after having begun to understand the larger order. Your previous unbalanced ways are now more painful. This Big Mind, sacred vision order compels you to listen. Your Small Mind ways always bring more pain. The larger, spiritual reality patiently awaits your awakening.

*All truths wait in all things. They neither hasten
their own delivery nor resist it.*
                                Walt Whitman
                                American Poet

It's up to you. Your path is there. If you wander off, it *is* possible to find it again. Not to worry. There will be many ways to find your way back to it. The system of the larger order is set up so that you must inevitably come to it many times in your life. You cannot avoid it. Your pain will drive you back. Books, poetry, the theatre, opera — all of these forms can take you back to the Way of Lessons. Moreover, you will find many interesting fellow travelers whose observations go beyond the limitations of the material world and serve as reminders. They may be a rabbi at a Bar Mitzvah or a farmer talking about the soil. Or, your enlightenment just might come from that dose of unresolved pain you've been thinking about while you've been reading.

As a kid, I loved to bail hay in Northern Indiana. We often worked late into the hot summer evenings to put it all up into the barn. A dairy farmer I worked for frequently had a problem with a reluctant lead cow that dallied and grazed along the lane. Her reluctance often caused the whole milking sequence to be delayed, making the regular chores more difficult in the busy harvest season. The farmer had a two-by-four with a carved handle that he called The Reminder. In the late summer evening, her bell would fall silent, and the farmer would get The Reminder and disappear down the lane. THWACK! MOOAWWW! You could hear her lesson repeated in the darkness.

It would have been so much easier for her if she could have remembered her lesson. I'm grateful that you have shared the opportunity, in these pages, to go beyond grazing and to recognize the wonder of our own natural relationship reminders.

A favorite poem of mine brings an additional natural perspective to our shared relationship work. It's a poem by Robert Frost called "A Tuft of Flowers." In the poem, Frost uses a pitchfork to turn hay that was cut earlier in the morning. He feels a subtle, but unexplainable connection with the fellow worker who had cut the hay. Yet, he couldn't see or hear him. Suddenly, a butterfly glides across the field and lights on a beautiful tuft of flowers standing by a stream that runs through the meadow. He realizes his companion left the flowers standing for their sheer natural beauty. He is, at that moment, enlightened. Through that particular butterfly he sees a world beyond comparison — a world beyond the limitations of pain and work — the natural higher order of reality to which we all respond. He sees the connection between those *particular* flowers and the *universal,* natural experience we all share. The flowers and butterfly are a metaphoric connection, a communication beyond language. The last line of the poem is:

> "Men work together," I told him from the heart,
> "Whether they work together or apart."

Through understanding our most difficult relationships, we can find the connections, the possibilities and the meaning in our lives. Through the connections, we can accept our deeper values. We can discover who we are.

GLOSSARY

Addiction: A compulsive and repetitive self-destructive pattern that is associated with some form of gratification or altered state of mind. It keeps the person from dealing with reality and the fear of change. Defensive patterns, like the LR or HV patterns, are gratifying because of their relative consistency over time. Addictive gratification is most often associated with fear of change. Addictions are characterized by loss of control, compulsive activity and continued behavior in spite of adverse consequences.

Aristotelian: The philosophy of Aristotle (Greek philosopher 384- 322 B.C.) upon which rested much of the historical development of science. He *separated* cause and effect, subject and object, rather than seeing them, as Einstein and others did, in an ongoing relationship along a continuum. His work, 2,300 years ago, was an effort to formulate a general method for scientific inquiry. His was an either/or, dualistic system of *defining categories.*

Attachment: The mental activity that results in a feeling of ownership. We use attachments to avoid change, because they provide apparent consistency. Attachments are often associated with dependencies. Preferences are choice-motivated, but attachments are beyond choice. People can become attached to their own defenses. Relationship attachment freezes the relationship itself, as well as each partner's individual development.

Balance/Balance Process: The natural means by which we all seek to grow and become wise. When it is successful we synchronize with the change at hand. When it is not practiced, we become frozen and create further pain. You were seeking balance long before you read this book or heard the term.

Big Mind: A term used to describe a conceptualization of life that includes everything you know or have experienced. It includes an awareness of the laws of nature —

of life, death, and change — as well as your reaction to these issues. It is an open-minded process term that contrasts with *Small Mind* (which is content-oriented and defensive).

Categorical: Dualistic, 100-percent thinking that attempts to categorize and pigeonhole. The feeling of safety one gets with categories derives from the illusion that they can be manipulated. Once categories are defined, people think they can avoid or control them. A category implies an absolute, 100-percent definition to which a negative or affirmative feeling can be attached. Categorical words include *all, always, never and only.* "You are always sick," and "You are a codependent," are both categorical remarks. Placing things in categories at first helps the decision-making process, but, ultimately, it inhibits it.

Codependent: Originally, the term described the partner of an individual who was dependent on mind-altering substances. Because the partner lived around the chemical, yet was not primarily addicted, he or she was considered "codependent" on the chemical. It is now a word that is working its way toward obsolescence. It could more usefully be replaced by the simple words "dependent" and "counterdependent," which are two forms of emotional dependency.

Comparisons: A quick clue to categorical, relapsive thinking. Using comparisons as a means of communicating is an example of prehistoric thinking.

Content: Aristotle was a content thinker. He looked at specifics and teased them apart. Content thinking avoids process and removes the element of change over time. It assumes that, once something is identified or codified, it is handled. It tacitly assumes that things don't change.

Detach: To emotionally disconnect from the relapsive process of emotional avoidance or control. To recognize one's limitations. The Serenity Prayer talks about detachment in the first line: *"... the serenity to accept the things I cannot change ..."* If you have trouble with the process of detaching, just remember the pain you have had with attachment. The pain will help you detach from your own will.

Diacritic: A form of thinking which is categorical, reductionist, and content-oriented. It is Aristotelian and caught up with the illusion that separating things into either "this" or "that" will continue to prove useful over time. Diacritic thinking is useful when you build a house or cross the street at a busy intersection. It is of limited value in relationship evolution.

Dualistic: Thought patterns which strike people and feelings into different either/or entities. It is neither necessary nor useful to think of a person as *either* an alcoholic *or* a codependent. An alcoholic *is* a dependent person. Problems can exist simultaneously. They don't necessarily arrive by coach after the previous problem has checked out.

Dysfunctional family: A negativistic, categorical term that provides built-in impediments to useful acceptance by those so labeled. No wonder critics are so irritated with the recovery movement. Who wants to be dysfunctional or from an impaired, dysfunctional family? It's another blow in a sea of negativity. But even the critics can admit they find themselves *out of balance* from time to time. And if they can't, then they are.

Einsteinian: Comprehensive thinking that involves field theory, imprecision and the acceptance of change. Words, and the things they represent, aren't limited by their placement in specific time. This type of thinking is *inclusive,* not *exclusive.* An Einsteinian view of relationship development is multi-dimensional. It isn't confined by static preconceptions or word labels.

Field Theory: The principles of both nuclear particle physics and recovery have similar characteristics as

Werner Heisenberg demonstrated in 1927. He found that one can't observe a nuclear particle precisely without changing its position. On the smallest level of measurement, there is no specific precision. Particles, therefore, exist in an imprecise area, a "field." In that "field" exist uncertainty and imprecision. So it is with relationships. Nothing is perfect. Nothing is static. Everything, on the most basic level, is constantly changing.

Helpless Victim: A disposable buzz word for frightened, dependent people who seek to control and manipulate others into caring for them and protecting them from reality. Through helplessness, they *control* relationships and *avoid* the outside world. They are addicted to the safety of a relationship. They disrespect themselves and excessively respect others. Their favorite affect is *sadness.* Their self-defeating attitude is one of *self-pity.*

Hero: One of the four subtypes of relationship patterns in which the person in question tends to be a LR in groups and a HV in personal relationships (LR/HV).

Impaired Family: A term that leaves the person or family in question feeling inappropriately victimized and defective *before* and *after* all of the relationship analyses. I suggest the alternative, less pejorative "family with balance issues." All families are unbalanced to some degree. Now, you don't have to call your family "impaired" to begin the recovery process.

Korzybski, Alfred 1879 - 1950: His magnum opus *Science and Sanity: An Introduction to Non-Aristotelian Systems and General Semantics* is a serious reference work for those more interested in thought and language in the recovery process. If you're a freshman in college, find this book. You can use it for every paper you will write from now until you graduate. Korzybski is the founder of the Field Theory of General Semantics, and he invented the concept of time-binding.

Lesson Process: Your most important lessons in life come from working through problems that arise in your most meaningful relationships. The lesson process exists as a natural phenomena, independent of our will to control or avoid it. *Deep Recovery* describes how you can use it for your own enlightenment.

Lone Ranger: A disposable buzz word for those who seek to *avoid* personal relationships and *control* those in the outside world. The original Lone Ranger discovered his life's mission in the throes of pain and victimhood. LR individuals feed their self-esteem by caretaking others. Their underlying dependency and pain is revealed in their counterdependent posturing. They have excessive respect for themselves and diminished respect for others. Their favorite affect is *anger.* Their self-defeating attitude is one of *pride.*

Lost Child: A subtype of relationship imbalance in which the person is a LR in both group and personal relationships. These people are such excessive Lone Rangers, that they often become victims (LR/LR).

Metaphoric View: Metaphors are inclusive and imprecise. No metaphor is categorically accurate, but they creatively connect disparate items or ideas. This book uses the principles of balanced recovery to metaphorically connect your relationship difficulties to physics, old songs, nature, humor and the mystical traditions of the American Indian.

Mascot: A subtype of relationship imbalance which is characterized by HV patterns in groups and LR patterns in personal relationships. No one really knows how the Mascot feels (HV/LR).

Natural Order: Our relationships follow a natural order of change that parallels the cycles of life and death witnessed, for example, in seasonal change. By understanding the instructions available in the natural order, we can harmonize our relationships and our lives.

Patterns: Obvious thoughts or behaviors repeated over time. They are often defensive and unbalanced. Balance requires fewer patterns and creative, spontaneous response to natural change. Discipline and balance reveal character and values. Defensive patterns don't.

Process: The way things happen over time, independent of the specific items in question. It's the "how" of something, the operational overview, rather than the content or the specifics in themselves. It's *how* the discussion takes place, not *what* the discussion was about.

Relapse: The process of returning to former patterns of self-victimization in order to cope with the changing world. People can relapse in their thinking, their words and, most frequently, in their relationships. Difficult relationships show you your attachments and often reveal unbalanced coping patterns. Through relationship relapse, you can discover how to remain in recovery.

Reductionistic: A way of thinking that reduces the variables in a situation so that certain items are excluded as being unimportant. Such thinking demonstrates an inability to cope with all aspects of reality. For example, it is reductionist to assume that because New York City has a "sophisticated" population, 1) everyone in New York City is sophisticated and 2) everyone else is not.

Scapegoat: The pattern of coping in which the person in question regularly sets victim roles for themselves in group and personal interaction. They often appear "rode hard and put up wet" (HV/HV).

Self: Your essential self consists of: 1) Good values that recognize your place in nature and the natural order; 2) your Cosmic Horn, an observation apparatus that can recognize unbalanced, destructive activities; and 3) Love, reflected in a drive to responsibly contribute to the enlightenment of others through respectful self-protection.

Self-Esteem: An awareness of appropriate self-mastery brings self-esteem. Maintaining balance in an unbalanced environment brings self-appreciation. Self-esteem is enhanced by ongoing connection with deep values and constructive contribution to the development of fellow humans. Lack of balance brings decreased self-esteem, because you know you're frightened and practicing avoidance or control.

Semantics: The branch of linguistics concerned with the nature, structure, development and changes in the meanings of speech forms and their influence on psychology and sociology (Webster's New Collegiate Dictionary).

Synesthetic: From "synesthesia" in psychology and neurology wherein stimulation of one part (color-eyes) will stimulate and reveal the connection with another receptor site (smell-nose). The different sensory sites of color and smell are connected. Synesthetic thinking is integrative and accepts connections that may not superficially appear to be present. Creative thinking is synesthetic.

Synergistic: The simultaneous action of separate agencies which together have greater total effect than the sum of their individual effects (Webster's New Collegiate Dictionary). Simultaneous recovery from both chemical dependency and psychological dependency patterns has a profound synergistic effect on the entire recovery process.

Transcendence: In philosophy, a reality above categories or predicaments (Webster's New Collegiate Dictionary). Relationship difficulties can lead to your transcendent path, as you detach from previous labels and predicaments to see the Big Picture. Relationship relapse is your spiritual awareness guide.

Universal Design: A term used by spiritual masters for thousands of years to designate the larger order of things. Recovery is a spiritual practice that keeps reminding us of the naturally occurring universal design. It is a process that includes, but goes beyond, content.

Values: When you start in recovery, your values are self-protective and deceptive. As you progress, they are more courageous, honest and selfless.

Victimhood: A buzz word that connotes the state of being a victim. Through your self-imposed victimhood you can learn balance. Through the principles of balance and self-responsibility, you will evolve with your relationship opportunities.

APPENDIX

GENERAL REFERENCE:

Science and Sanity: An Introduction to non-Aristotelian Systems and General Semantics by Alfred Korzybski. This book is a valuable reference for everything from psychology and semantics to philosophy and quantum mechanics. Korzybski is an integrative genius and visionary. It isn't a book you should expect to read at one sitting, but rather to work your way through over the years. Available from The Institute of General Semantics, Lakeville, Connecticut. (If you don't wish to go into Korzybski in such depth, I suggest *Symbol Status and Personality* by S.I. Hayakawa.)
ISBN 0-937298-01-8   806 pages, hardcover $23.50

SELF-MANAGEMENT:

The Art of War (The Art of Strategy) by Sun Tzu and translated by Thomas Cleary. Written by a Chinese Warrior General over 2,000 years ago. The relationship principles are timeless, interesting and practically useful. This Cleary translation from Shambala Press is the best. It not only has comments from "Master Sun," but eleven other interpreters of the original text.
ISBN 0-87773-452-6   172 pages, paperback $9.95

Shambala: The Sacred Path of the Warrior by Chogyam Trungpa. This interesting book addresses the issue of natural wisdom and balance in a way not often explored by the recovering community. The first book of the Shambala series, it is essential for advanced leadership evolution.
ISBN 0-394-72329-5   199 pages, paperback $6.95

MEDITATION:

Seeking the Heart of Wisdom: The Path of Insight Meditation by Joseph Goldstein and Jack Kornfeld. I cannot emphasize enough the importance of meditation as an essential activity in the recovery process. This book, complete and readable, is a practical, how-to-get-started book for those interested in essential recovery adventures

through meditation.
ISBN 0-87773-327-9 195 pages, paperback $10.95

Zen Mind, Beginners Mind by Shunryu Suzuki. This book is a must if you're undertaking a path of insight meditation. Even if you don't meditate, however, the simple truths in this book are priceless.
ISBN 0-8348-0079-9 138 pages, paperback $3.95

The Ring of the Way: Testament of a Zen Master by Taisen Deshimaru. This is a practical and useful book written by a highly evolved martial artist and Zen Master. It will keep you focused on the essential truths of the recovery process.
ISBN 0-525-48293-8 130 pages, paperback $8.95

The Secret Path: A Modern Technique for Self-Discovery by Dr. Paul Brunton. This is another practical book that emphasizes meditation as a means to find your own true nature and to release yourself from destructive attachments. Brunton has written many books on spiritual issues.
ISBN 0-87728-652-3 128 pages, paperback $5.95

ADDITIONAL RECOMMENDATIONS:
Maps of the Mind: Charts and Concepts of the Mind and Its Labyrinths by Charles Hampden-Turner
ISBN 0-02-547740-4 224 pages, $14.95 hardback

The Denial of Death by Ernst Becker
ISBN 0-02-902380-7 314 pages, $8.95 paperback

The Mind of Clover: Essays on Zen Ethics by Robert Aitken
ISBN 0-86547-158-4 199 pages, $11.50 paperback

Symbol Status and Personality by S.I. Hayakawa
ISBN 0-15-687611-6 188 pages, $5.95 paperback

Chop Wood and Carry Water: A Guide to Finding Spiritual Fulfillment in Everyday Life by Fields, Taylor, Weyler, Ingrasci.
ISBN 0-874-77209-5 287 pages, $11.95 paperback

The Sword of No Sword: Life of the Master Warrior Tesshu by John Stevens
ISBN 0-394-72770-3 167 pages, $9.95 paperback

The Kingdom Within: The Inner Meaning of Jesus' Sayings by John A. Sanford
ISBN 0-8091-2329-0 226 pages, $6.95 paperback

A Book of Five Rings: The Classic Guide to Strategy by Miyamoto Musashi
ISBN 0-87951-153-2 95 pages, $9.95 paperback (Overlook Press)

Six Thinking Hats: An Approach to Business Management by Edward deBono
ISBN 0-316-17791-1 207 pages, $16.95 hardback

No Boundary: Eastern and Western Approaches to Personal Growth by Ken Wilbur
ISBN 0-394-7488-1-6 160 pages, $7.95 paperback

The Way of the Peaceful Warrior: A Book that Changes Lives by Dan Millman
ISBN 0-915811-00-6 210 pages, $9.95 paperback

Steps to an Ecology of Mind by Gregory Bateson
ISBN 0-87668-950-0 545 pages, $40.00

Everyday Zen: Love and Work by Charlotte Joko Beck
ISBN 0-06-060734-3 214 pages, $9.95 paperback

Zen and the Art of Motorcycle Maintenance: An Inquiry into Values by Robert Pirsig
ISBN 0-553-25748-x 416 pages, $4.95 paperback

The Tao of Physics by Fritjof Capra
ISBN 0-553-14206-2 332 pages, $3.95 paperback

The Reality Illusion: How You Make the World You Experience by Ralph Strauch
ISBN 0-88268-079-x 202 pages, $10.95 paperback

INDEX

OTHER PRODUCTS BY DR. CHARLES PARKER

Dr. Parker has also produced two interesting and entertaining audio learning systems that can contribute to your recovery efforts. These systems can be ordered through the order form on the last page.

KNOWING YOUR SELF: Essential Guidelines for Learning from Your Own Life. Six one-hour cassettes that discuss many aspects of a balanced recovery process. $39.95

1. "Growing Up and Letting Go: Sources of Addiction in the Family." How our problems start with patterns programed in from childhood and what you can do to resolve them.

2. "Drugs, Sports and the Illusion of Winning." How every day experience in the competition of sports can reveal the principles of balance and thereby contribute to recovery.

3. "Painful Bonds: The Nature of Destructive Relationships." How your most important relationships can become unbalanced and difficult, and what you can do when that happens.

4. "Your Identity and Your Job: Understanding the Personal Sacrifices." How the work group also offers abundant relationship difficulties and opportunities for self-awareness.

5. "Caring Too Much and Not Caring Enough: Reasonable Rules in Personal Relationships." How to set boundaries and achieve emotional balance in your most important relationships.

6. "Rebuilding from Within: Making Room for Spirituality." How to use spirituality as a valuable tool in your recovery process.

FROM BEDROOM TO BOARDROOM: How to Improve Your Most Important Relationships. Two one-hour cassettes that summarize relationship difficulties and outline a specific recovery plan. $19.95

1. "How We Create Our Own Relationship Problems." How, from earliest history, we have set ourselves up by our own unbalanced defensiveness. Learn how frozen LR or HV patterns can teach us essential lessons from our most important relationships.

2. "What We Can Do to Resolve Our Relationship Problems." How to use balance concepts, your own integrated feelings and the RAPIDS process to become truly responsible with yourself.

Recovery program consultations, hospital management training seminars and a variety of other self and group management presentations by Dr. Parker are available. To discuss your specific needs, please contact:

The Parker Group
168 Business Park Drive
Virginia Beach, Virginia 23462
Toll Free: (800) 477-3750

ORDER FORM

Telephone Orders: Call toll free 1-800-477-3750 and have your VISA or MasterCard ready.

FAX Orders: (804) 473-3768

Postal Orders: Hawkeye Press
P.O. Box 62547
Virginia Beach, VA 23462

Please send the following books or audio cassette learning systems. I understand that I may return any item for a full refund of the purchase price if I am dissatisfied for any reason.

	Quantity	Price per Item	Total
DEEP RECOVERY	_____	$12.95 U.S.	_____
	_____	$15.95 Canada	_____
KNOWING YOUR SELF	_____	$39.95 U.S.	_____
(6 audio cassettes)	_____	$49.95 Canada	_____
BEDROOM TO	_____	$19.95 U.S.	_____
BOARDROOM	_____	$24.95 Canada	_____
(2 audio cassettes)			

SUB-TOTAL   _____

SALES TAX: Please add 4½% in Virginia   _____

SHIPPING: $2.00 for the first item and
75¢ for each additional item
(include an additional $1.00
per item shipped to Canada).   _____

TOTAL DUE   _____

___ Please add my name to Dr. Parker's mailing list for information on new publications and audio systems.

PAYMENT:
___ Check (made payable to Hawkeye Press)
___ VISA   ___ MasterCard

Card Number:
_____

Cardholder's Name:
_____

Expiration Date:
_____

SHIP TO:
Name: _____
Address: _____
City: _____
State: _____ Zip _____

ABOUT THE AUTHOR

Dr. Charles Parker is a child and adult psychiatrist, a psychoanalyst and a certified addiction specialist. As executive medical director, he has been instrumental in the development of highly successful chemical dependency and codependency programs at HCA Peninsula Hospital in Hampton, VA. These programs treat patients from throughout the United States and Canada and have, in fact, been used as models by other institutions.

Dr. Parker is still in active private practice as the medical director of the Center for Personal Recovery in Virginia Beach, VA, an outpatient facility for the treatment of chemical dependency, codependency and other psychiatric disorders. Additionally, he is president of the Parker Group, a hospital management and consulting firm.

His unusually extensive training, along with a diverse clinical and administrative background, make Dr. Charles Parker one of the most important new writers in the recovery field today.